BUTTERFLIES ON MY MIND

Small Copper and Wall butterflies.

DULCIE GRAY

BUTTERFLIES ON MY MIND

Their Life and Conservation in Britain Today

illustrated by Brian Hargreaves

Foreword by Sir Peter Scott

ANGUS & ROBERTSON · PUBLISHERS

ANGUS & ROBERTSON · PUBLISHERS
Brighton · Sydney · Melbourne · Singapore · Manila

First published by Angus & Robertson (UK) Ltd,
16, Ship Street, Brighton, in 1978

Illustrations © Brian Hargreaves 1978

Maps © Institute of Terrestrial Ecology 1978
Prepared by the Biological Records Centre, Monks Wood
Experimental Station under contract to the
Nature Conservancy Council

ISBN 0 207 95804 1

Typeset by HBM Typesetting Ltd, Chorley, Lancs
Printed in Great Britain by Hazell Watson & Viney Ltd,
Aylesbury, Bucks

CONTENTS

Chapter notes are indicated by superior figures (^{1}) in the text.

All illustrations are life-size unless otherwise indicated.

ACKNOWLEDGEMENTS

I would respectfully like to thank Her Majesty the Queen for allowing me to visit Buckingham Palace Garden in February 1977 to discuss its butterfly population with the Head Gardener, Mr Nutbeam.

When Dr Charles Lane, now an embryologist with the Medical Research Council, was aged eight, his mother, Dr Miriam Rothschild, the celebrated flea expert and lepidopterist, suggested he might watch migrant moths and butterflies crossing the Channel at Trouville, where the family was on holiday. His acknowledgements in the paper he produced, which was printed in the *Entomologist's Monthly Magazine*, began like this: 'I should like to thank my mother for writing down this account for me (and whoever corrected her spelling).'

My spelling is fair, but the friendliness I have been shown and the help I have received from distinguished and very busy entomologists while writing this book are something I shall never forget.

Three people have been so remarkable that I am forced to mention them first: Mr John Heath, the entomologist in charge of Insect Distribution Mapping in the Biological Records Centre at the Institute of Terrestrial Ecology at Monks Wood, with whom I made a rough plan of the book, and who has read the entire manuscript for me; Mr N. D. Riley, for twenty-three years Keeper of Entomology at the British Museum (and whose book *A Field Guide to the Butterflies of Britain and Europe*, written in conjunction with Dr L. G. Higgins, is recognized as an outstanding contribution to the subject), who read the first draft and who reacted to it so kindly, and amended it with such care and tact, that I felt I had been given a birthday present; and Mr Robert Goodden of Worldwide Butterflies, to whom I turned in moments of stress, and who never failed me.

I should also like to thank Dr Miriam Rothschild; Professor Fred Urquhart, the famous 'Monarch' expert of Scarborough College, University of Toronto, Canada; Dr Michael Morris and Dr Jeremy Thomas of Furzebrook Research Station; Dr J. P. Dempster, Dr Eric Duffey, Dr Ernest Pollard and Miss Lynne Farrell, of Monks Wood; Dr Robert Pyle, Chairman of the Lepidoptera Specialist Group of the Survival Service Commission of the International Union for the Conservation of Nature, and founder of the Xerces Society; the Reverend A. H. H. Harbottle; and, in the Department of Entomology of the British Museum (Natural History), Mr R. I. Vane-Wright, Dr J. D. Bradley (Lepidoptera Specialist, Commonwealth Institute), Miss Pamela Gilbert (Librarian), Mr D. J. Carter (Lepidoptera section), and Mr J. E. Chainey; Mr W. G. Tremewen, Editor of the *Entomologist's Gazette;* Mr Roy French of Rothamsted Experimental Station; Dr H. G. Heal of Queen's University, Belfast; Mr Robert Nash of the Ulster Museum, Botanic Gardens, Belfast; Colonel A. M. Emmet; the late Mr Denzil Ffennell, the Entomological Recorder for Hampshire and the Isle of Wight; Professor Brian Blakey of McMaster University, Hamilton, Canada; Mr Torben B. Larsen; and Miss Molly Cox of the BBC, and to let them know how greatly I feel in their debt.

I also wish to thank the Hon. Mrs Elspeth Hoare; Miss Elizabeth Cartwright; Mr Martin Amis; Mr Peter Macdonald of the Canadian Broadcasting Company, Ottawa, Canada, and his wife Fran; Miss Roseanne Newman of the Entomology Library at the Experiment Farm in Ottawa; and Miss Barbara Irwin of the Science and Technology Section of the Metropolitan Library, Toronto, for their help and kindness; and last but far from least, the well-known entomologist, writer and butterfly photographer, Mr George Hyde, of Bessacarr, Yorkshire, who was the first person to encourage me to write a book on butterflies, and Mr Thomas Frankland, who ten years ago did me the honour of asking me to become a Vice President of the British Butterfly Conservation Society.

To Michael Denison, my husband, goes a very special debt of gratitude. For the entire time I was writing this book, he was interested and encouraging, and asked just the kind of questions that it was specifically designed to answer.

FOREWORD

by Sir Peter Scott

This book has a serious purpose – to describe and display the beauty and variety of British butter-flies, and to encourage the reader to play a part in their conservation. Like myself, the author prefers her butterflies on the wing – alive, rather than in a cabinet drawer – and her book, en-hanced by Brian Hargreaves's beautiful, accurate and lively illustrations, reflects this attitude to her subject.

Hers is an enviably light touch, but butterflies *are* on her mind, and her mind is by no means frivolous. She has consulted the authorities, past and present, and has received from the latter, as she gratefully acknowledges, encouragement on a scale which is a credit both to them and to her.

Not the least of her achievements is that much of what she has learned from many specialists is assembled for the first time within the covers of a single book. Even more important for the general reader, the fruits of this research are presented attractively and personally. Her theatrical instinct for apparently effortless communication has served her subject well. *Butterflies on my Mind* has my enthusiastic welcome.

INTRODUCTION

Butterflies are beautiful. They contribute colour and liveliness to the spring, summer and autumn scenes; next to the bees and moths they are the most efficient of the flower pollinators, and in this country, except for the caterpillars of the Large White and Small White (sometimes known as the 'cabbage whites', from their habit of feeding on cabbages), they are not destructive in any way. Unfortunately this does not guarantee their survival.

I have loved them ever since I can remember, and would like to be able to pass on a little of my love and enthusiasm to others.

This book is about British butterflies, and is written primarily for those who are worried about their decline, and interested in what is being done to preserve them and sometimes to reintroduce from abroad species which have become extinct in Britain.

I am not writing for professionals, nor for amateur experts (and in this field many amateurs are very knowledgeable), but for those who want to learn a little more about butterflies in a reasonably simple but accurate manner. I make no claim that I am an expert. I am not. My wish is only to share information I have received from those more knowledgeable than myself about a subject that I believe and hope is becoming of increasing interest to people in these islands.

This book is therefore a personal voyage of discovery for me through seas long familiar on the surface, which on closer inspection have yielded up many unsuspected wonders. Its plan – if that is not too rigid a word for such an adventure – is a consideration, in three broad sections, of man's relationship with this most beautiful of insects: first, the slow growth of his knowledge, his passion for collection and for changing the environment, his belated awareness of the consequences of his actions and certain attempts to put matters right; second, a brief look at the butterfly's varied roles in world myths and religions; and lastly, a review of common or garden butterflies, and of the men and women who work with such unobtrusive dedication in research and conservation, and some suggestions as to how even the least scientific among us can help.

There seems at last, and not before time, to be a feeling that man should make a conscious effort to co-exist with wild nature. In some places irreparable damage has been done; in others perhaps rescue is possible. If by writing this book I have made even one more person care about the conservation of British butterflies, then my efforts will not have been in vain.

To Marie Ney
With love

'Le papillon est une fleur qui vole,
La fleur un papillon fixé.'

Econchard Lebrun,
Epigrammes, VI, 87.

DISCOVERY

When the then famous film star, Robert Taylor, came over from America to England in 1938 to star in a film called *A Yank at Oxford*, a young English actor, Tony Halfpenny, played the cox in the boat race scene. His mother, who was a keen fan, asked her son to be sure and tell her the first words Mr Taylor said to him. Naturally Tony agreed, and he waited eagerly. Robert Taylor settled himself down in the boat which was rocking on the choppy water, and said, 'Jesus, Cox, I've got butterflies in my belly.'

I know what he meant, though for me the meaning is slightly different. I have had a passion for British butterflies since I was four years old. I can clearly remember the first time I became aware of them. It was in the long, narrow garden of a house our family had rented, at Cooden in Sussex. An uncle and aunt and two girl cousins were staying with us for a holiday. I had just been brought to England from Malaysia where I was born, and was getting to know my brother and sister and these other relatives for the first time. Some of the children were older than I, and were catching large butterflies from a mauve bush, and putting them into jam jars to die. I can see, even now, those sad wings flapping, and the struggles to live becoming feebler, and feebler.

There are numerous wonderful butterflies in Malaysia, so why they hadn't impinged on me I don't know, but it is still British butterflies which interest me most; perhaps because I know a little more about them.

For the next few years I went to boarding school in Wallingford, and there we were allowed to collect birds' eggs, though not encouraged to chase butterflies. I myself collected live snails at this time, and let them loose in the cloakroom – I liked the multi-coloured trails of slime they left behind them. I also found a hen's claw with the tendon intact so that it could still make the claw contract, and I took it to bed with me when I was lonely. In retrospect, I am glad that I didn't then collect butterflies, because it is with conservation that I am now concerned. At a holiday home in Norfolk, however, where I was sent because my parents lived abroad, I did make a collection, and I also began to learn about the various species, and to become interested in this very variety. Of course, no two butterflies are exactly alike, any more than two human beings are, but within the different species the individuals are alike enough to be indistinguishable to all but the most ardent student!

There are seventy species of butterfly classed as British, and of these only fifty-nine breed in this country, and only fifty-seven 'overwinter'. The rest, which include the Queen of Spain Fritillary and the three Clouded Yellows, are migrants. Some of them travel enormous distances, like the Monarch or Milkweed butterfly from North America, the Painted Lady which comes from Africa, and the Camberwell Beauty which crosses the North Sea.

Of the million or so species of animals known to exist, about eight hundred thousand are insects, and these have only been classified (and not all yet) during the past two or three hundred years. Before that, insects (except the obviously useful ones like bees or silkworms) were generally regarded as pests. In fact there is still in existence a 4,000-year-old Egyptian papyrus that lists ways and means of getting rid of lice, fleas and wasps; though in a splendid fresco of around 1400 BC from the tomb of Nebamum in Thebes (now a part of Luxor) there is a scene called 'Fowling in the Marshes', in which seven specimens of *Danaus chrysippus*, the African version of the Monarch butterfly, are clearly and beautifully portrayed. The fresco is on display at the British Museum.[1]

Before the end of the fifteenth century, the great voyages of discovery had begun; and ever since, expeditions have returned with samples of flora and fauna. After the fall of Constantinople in 1453, the learning of the ancients which had so long been a guarded secret there was brought to the West by the scholars who had managed to escape the destruction of the city. Increased contact with such scholars and the simultaneous invention of printing gave enormous impetus to the study of Greek science and natural history; but until the seventeenth century, when a usable kind of microscope was invented, the study of insects was very rudimentary. Most scientists still thought that insects and grubs arrived spontaneously in any dark corner, or pile of dirt, or from rotting animal flesh.[2] The microscope provided the breakthrough for the 'minute scientists' as those who studied insects were called. Even Galileo (1564–1642) became fascinated, saying, 'With infinite wonder I have examined very many minute creatures among which the most horrible are the fleas, and the most beautiful ants and moths.'

As James Duncan, the nineteenth-century entomologist, wrote: 'It was long a general belief that butterflies underwent at each successive stage a complete transmutation or change from one being to another. Such an opinion presented no difficulties to those who like Virgil imagined that a swarm of honey bees might be generated from a piece of putrid flesh, or like Kircher that a crop of serpents might be reared from cut pieces of snakes, roasted and sown in an "oleaginous soil". Even Izaak Walton [1593–1683] approved the theory of Pliny the Younger [the historian who gave such a vivid eye-witness account of the eruption of Vesuvius] that many caterpillars have their birth or being from a dew that in the Spring falls upon the leaves of trees.'

And one of the most learned men of the Middle Ages, the Dominican Dr Universalis, known as Albertus Magnus (1206–80), who was tutor to St Thomas Aquinas, believed that caterpillars, which he supposed laid eggs, and butterflies, which he called 'winged worms, various coloured', were entirely unrelated.[3]

James Duncan goes on: 'The accurate investigations of Malpighi and Swammerdam were the first to show the subject in a true light by demonstrating in what the transformation of butterflies essentially consists.'

Because of the work scientists have done before us, we now take for granted as common knowledge the fact that the butterfly starts as an egg, which hatches out into a caterpillar, which turns into a chrysalis, from which the butterfly itself emerges. But if this had never been proved to us, just imagine our amazement and disbelief when faced with the suggestion that one single creature should undergo such dramatic changes. Unless we had been fortunate enough actually to have observed this process of metamorphosis, we surely would have been as baffled as people were in less enlightened times! (There is a short description of a caterpillar turning into a chrysalis in Appendix 1.)

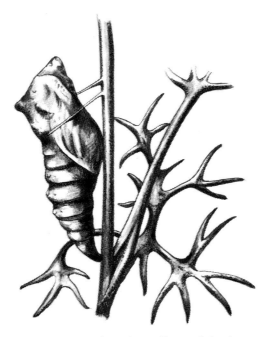

Chrysalis of Swallowtail (x 2).

Marcello Malpighi (1628–94) made discoveries so important in the realm of animal and vegetable structure that he may be considered to be the founder of microscopic anatomy, but his subjects included frogs, the human lung and the brain, rather than butterflies. It was left to Johannis (christened Jan) Jacob Swammerdam (1637–80), a Dutchman from a wealthy background, to discover by dissection that 'the skins of the caterpillar and the chrysalis are enveloped in each other, as is also the butterfly with all its organs, but these in a fluid stage'. He had previously studied medicine, with the encouragement of his father, specializing in anatomy, but he became so obsessed with insects that his health suffered through overwork. In Hill's *The Book of Nature, or the History of Insects*, 1758, the scientist Boerhaave, who wrote the Introduction, gave the following description of Swammerdam's obsession: 'He ransacked with this view, the air, the land and the water, fields, meadows, pastures corn grown, downs, wastes, sandhills, rivers, ponds, wells, lakes, seas, and their shores and banks, trees, plants, ruins, caves, uninhabited places, and even bog-houses in search of Eggs, Worms, Nymphs, and Butterflies.'

At the same time Swammerdam quarrelled with his parents, who cut off his allowance, leaving him penniless. Some of his works were published during his lifetime, but for others he didn't have the money to pay the printers. Later, he developed religious mania, and though on the death of his father he once again became comfortably-off by selling his father's 'curiosities' (in effect a natural history museum), he lived the rest of his life in religious contemplation. He left his manuscripts – some of the early works were on medicine – to Prince Melchisidec Thévenot, whom he met while studying medicine by the Loire. Thévenot was formerly King's Minister at Geneva. On his death they passed into the hands of Boerhaave, who eventually published them.

Due to his breakdown and his religious mania, Swammerdam's great work, *Historia Insectorum Generalis*, published in 1669, only two years after he obtained his degree in medicine, was not believed. Three years later it was published in French, under the title *Histoire des Insectes*, with the sub-title (here given in English), 'In which is clearly revealed the slow and almost imperceptible manner of the growth of their wings, and in which is exposed beyond doubt the error of the commonly accepted theory of their so-called transformation.'

He wrote: 'The History I am about to give, is so amazing in all its circumstances, that it might very well pass for romance, were it not the most firm truth. We shall see most surprising changes in the limbs of these insects, such changes as no human wit could ever think of. Behold a poor and wretched insect lose by degrees all motion, and in appearance stand consigned to death; in which seemingly hopeless condition, however, all its former wings acquire such an extraordinary degree of perfection, until at last, rising in the gaiety of most resplendent colours, it no longer continues a reptile of foul appearance creeping upon the earth, but now flies freely through the air attracting our admiration by its most elegant shape and clothing . . .

'The whole operation consists in this, that the chrysalis casts its skin, and shows the parts which have hitherto lain concealed, unfolds its limbs, and arranges each in its right place with great regularity and order . . . It is clearly and distinctly seen that within the skin of the chrysalis, a perfect and real butterfly is hidden, and therefore the skin of the chrysalis must be considered only as an outer garment, containing in it, parts belonging to the nature of a butterfly, which have grown under its defence by slow degrees, in like manner as other sensitive bodies increase by accretion.'

He was a true man of science, using specially designed scissors and knives so tiny that they had to be sharpened under a microscope; but he knew that it would be an uphill struggle to wean his readers from their easy addiction to myth and legend. 'We sit down contentedly in our studies,' he wrote, 'and feed ourselves with our weak fancies, instead of looking for the truth into the magnificent works of the Creator, though such inspection alone can give us just notice of what we desire to know.' It is sad that he was discounted by his contemporaries.

Painted Ladies (male) on thistle.

There is evidence that metamorphosis was recognized by some Greeks and Romans, though they were without benefit of scientific research. Nevertheless, as late as 1634 it was held to be merely imaginary in Britain. Sir Theodore de Mayerne (about whom more later) didn't believe it, and said, 'If animals are to be transmuted, so may metals.'

The ancients made many allusions to the wonderful changes which the insect tribes undergo, and built a number of their fictions on them. The mythological story of Eros/Cupid and Psyche is an allegory of the human soul, and of love, sexual and spiritual. Psyche in Greek signifies the soul, and is frequently represented as a butterfly, not only because of the beauty of the insect, but because of its resurrection from seeming death at the chrysalis stage. The ancient Greek word for butterfly was in fact *psyche*.

In a passage which is a happy blend of fact, faith, and nineteenth-century prose James Duncan wrote: 'With greatly more accurate notions of the real nature of the transformation, few modern writers on the subject have failed to notice and dilate upon the general symbolical analogy, which subsists between this, and the changes which the human body is destined to undergo. The caterpillar, chiefly occupied for its bodily wants and appetites, is regarded as representing the ordinary condition of human life; the chrysalis the intermediate state of death, and the perfect animal, the renovated body, when it rises from the tomb to enter upon a more exalted state of existence . . . And here the parallel holds perfectly true between insect and man. The butterfly, the representative of the soul, is prepared in the larva for its future state of glory; and if it be not destroyed by ichneumen and other enemies to which it is exposed, symbolical of the vices that destroy the spiritual life of the soul, it will come to its state of repose in the pupa which is its Hades, and at length when it assumes the imago, break forth with new power and beauty, to its final glory and reign of love.'

The first person to be believed on the subject of metamorphosis was a woman, Maria Sybilla Merian. She was born in Frankfurt-am-Main in 1647, the only daughter of two German artists. Her father was an engraver who died when she was four, and her mother married again. The second husband was also an artist, Jacob Marrel, a well-known painter of the 'School of Utrecht', one of the schools of German and Dutch flower artists which flourished at this time.[4] The Utrecht school was chiefly distinguished for its use of insects in flower pictures. Maria worked in Marrel's studio as a child, and was taught how to paint flowers, and also miniatures (because these were very commercial). She was a great help to the family, but when sent out to collect the flowers to paint, she would also collect caterpillars, and this was frowned on as unladylike. Jacob Marrel used to take her with him to do field work, and of this her mother also disapproved.

When she was eighteen she married a painter called Johann Graff, and they went to live in Nuremberg. They had two daughters, Joanna and Dorothea, but the marriage was unhappy.

Maria became interested in a fanatical religious sect called the Labadists whose creed stated 'Man is nothing', and she took her children with her to live in one of their communes at Castle Bosch in Friesland. The Labadists didn't believe in marriage or property. Her husband tried to persuade her to come back to him in 1686, but she refused, and never lived with him again. She resumed the name of Merian, and even made a will, calling herself a widow, although Johann didn't die until 1701.

To earn a living for herself and her daughters, she did embroidery, and invented a special way of painting flowers directly on to tablecloths, using vegetable dyes made by herself, and painting different patterns on the back and front of the cloth; and became so well known for it that it is said she decorated the tent of an army general in this manner. Like many of the intellectuals of her time, she was fascinated by Surinam in South America, having heard of the beauties of its flora and fauna. There is no space here to describe her travels there, but because of her fame English entomologists were still including butterflies from Surinam in their books in the nineteenth century. She also published a book called *The New Flower Book*, which was a tremendous success. Encouraged, she produced a second, which was called *The Wonderful Formation of Caterpillars and Their Strange Diet of Flowers*.

In her Introduction she says: 'From my earliest childhood I studied insects. I began in Frankfurt by observing silkworms, and then having noted that all beautiful butterflies and night moths grew out of caterpillars, I collected as many as I could find, and learned to draw them so faithfully that I hope it will satisfy the Natural philosophers. I do this for the glory of God, as without Him I would never have undertaken the work, much less allowed myself to be persuaded to print it; especially as being a woman, with little time left over after taking care of my household, this work might be mistaken as "unseemly ambition".' She described the chrysalides of the Swallow-tail caterpillar in this charming way: 'They have a form very much like a child in swaddling clothes.'

She died almost destitute. Both Carl Linné, the great Swedish naturalist, who was very nearly her contemporary, and Goethe, who as well as being Germany's most famous poet was a scientist and natural philosopher of some repute, thought very highly of her work. (Goethe was also born in Frankfurt-am-Main, but nearly a hundred years after Maria.)

In this country, the first person to publish a treatise on insects was a physician to King Charles I, Sir Theodore de Mayerne (the man who didn't believe in metamorphosis), in 1634. He edited it, and wrote the Introduction; the treatise, *Insectorum sive Minimorum Animalium Theatrum etc*, was by T. Moffett (variously called Muffet, Mouffet and Moufet, and referred to elsewhere in this book, especially in connection with *The History of Animals, Serpents, etc* which, as Muffet, he wrote with Edward Topsel). An English translation was published in 1658, and for the first time in any book on entomology included sixteen species of British butterfly.[5] In 1666 Christopher Merrett wrote a book which included twenty-one species, one of which seems to have been the Purple-edged Copper, which certainly doesn't exist here now, and hasn't for a long time. In 1790 John Ray wrote *Historia Insectorum*, which included forty-eight of our species, and in 1720 Eleazar Albin published the first book giving coloured illustrations. It is called *A Natural History of English Insects*, and the illustrations were hand-painted by himself; I have a copy. (I bought it from Phyllis Calvert's husband, Peter Murray Hill, who alas died very young, with the first money I made from films.)

On 1 January 1758 came an event of enormous importance to all students of butterflies. Carl Linné (1707–78), usually known as Linnaeus because he wrote in Latin and called himself Carolus Linnaeus, published the tenth edition of his *Systema Naturae*, in which he introduced the binominal system of nomenclature which is still used throughout the world today. Each butterfly was given two Latin names, the first indicating its general attributes (genus), and the second its special characteristics (species). The Large Blue, for instance, is known as *Maculinea arion*, and the Purple Hairstreak as *Quercusia quercus*.

Two more works published in the eighteenth century are worth a mention here: Benjamin Wilkes's great work, *One Hundred and Twenty Copperplates of English Moths and Butterflies*, 1773, and *The Aurelian*, by Moses Harris, 1776. (This book, one of the most famous of all butterfly books, takes its name from the now obsolete term for a lepidopterist.[6])

In the nineteenth century, Edward Newman's *British Butterflies* demands mention; and in the twentieth, five great books of reference are R. South's *British Butterflies*, 1906, F. W. Frohawk's *Natural History of British Butterflies*, in two volumes, 1913 and 1924, E. B. Ford's *Butterflies*, 1945, L. G. Higgins's and N. D. Riley's *A Field Guide to the Butterflies of Britain and Europe*, 1970, and in 1973, T. G. Howarth's revision of South, *South's British Butterflies*.

All these books were written primarily for amateur collectors, but also to meet the needs of most scientific lepidopterists. For beginners whose first concern is to identify each species of British butterfly in an easy manner, I suggest H. D. Swain's excellent identification chart, published by Frederick Warne & Co Ltd in 1970. After all, if you are going to conserve your butterfly, you might as well know him when you see him.

You might as well distinguish him from a moth, too. I am so often questioned on the difference between a butterfly and a moth that I shall take this opportunity to give the following reasonably uncomplicated guide.

Orange Tips on meadow lady's smock and Brimstones on alder buckthorn.
(For detailed identification see key on p. 22.)

All British butterflies have clubbed antennae. Among our moths, the Red and Bottle Green Burnets have them. Butterflies always fly by day, and usually in sunshine. The Burnet moths also fly by day, but in other ways are far removed from butterflies. The Skipper family of butterflies (Hesperiidae) has the closest link with moths: for instance the caterpillars (or larvae[7]) of the Skippers have a moth-like habit of living in hiding, and rolling themselves up in leaves or blades of grass spun together. The chrysalides (or pupae[8]) are not suspended or supported as with other butterflies (the Small Skipper envelops itself in a silken cocoon); they differ, too, from other butterflies in their flight and posture, several of them assuming resting positions more suggestive of moths than other butterflies (for example, the Dingy Skipper rests at night exactly like a moth). Finally, in the case of the Chequered Skipper, the antennae, though clubbed, end in a point called the apiculus. But by and large, butterflies fly by day and have clubbed antennae, and moths (with the exception of the Burnets) don't have clubbed antennae, and more usually fly by night. There are also over two thousand three hundred British moths, to the meagre seventy British butterflies.

Notes

1. An article called 'Three and a Half Millenia of *Danaus chrysippus* L. (Lepidoptera Danaidae) in Upper Egypt' by Torben B. Larsen was published in *Linnéana Belgica*, Vol 7, 1977.

2. Eleazar Albin, writing in 1720 about Francisco Redi (1626–98), a celebrated naturalist, says: 'I have not met with one Instance, that gave me Reason to doubt of *Insects* in general being produced by Animal Parents of the same Species . . . I cannot help admiring how he, an ingenious *Italian* who wrote a treatise on the Subject, and so exact an Observer of Nature, could be led into so great a mistake as that some *Insects* were the Product of those *Vegetables* in whose Excrescences they had been nursed up.'

3. Aristotle (384–322 BC) also was peculiarly ill-informed on the subject of butterflies. He believed that they laid little worms, and that 'they take their colour from the worm they are bred of' (quoted in *The History of Animals, Serpents, etc*, by Edward Topsel and T. Muffet, 1658).

4. A picture by Marrel, once owned by Prince Littler, the theatrical impresario, was sold at Christie's in 1977 for £10,000.

5. From the descriptions these butterflies are thought to be the Speckled Wood, Wall, Dark Green Fritillary, Red Admiral, Painted Lady, Small Tortoiseshell, Large Tortoiseshell, Peacock, Comma, Common Blue, Green-veined White, Orange Tip, Clouded Yellow, Brimstone, Swallowtail and Silver-spotted Skipper.

6. Chambers Dictionary gives the following: '*Aurelia*, a common genus of jellyfishes: formerly a chrysalis, from its golden colour. Adjective *Aurelian*, golden: of an Aurelia. Also noun (obsolete) a lepidopterist.'

7. 'Larva' comes from the Latin, meaning 'a mask'; Linnaeus considered the real insect in that condition was under a mask.

8. 'Pupa' comes from the Latin, meaning 'a girl' or 'a doll'.

Key to illustration on p. 21
1 & 3: Orange Tip (male); 2: Orange Tip (female);
4: Brimstone (male); 5: Brimstone (female)

ENEMIES AND DEFENCES

Butterflies have many enemies, including man.[1] In fact man probably does more damage than most of the rest put together, though violent climatic changes, wasps, spiders and birds do their fair share. So do mice and hedgehogs, who catch butterflies when they are at rest.[2]

When I was a child I used to dislike singing the hymn 'From Greenland's Icy Mountains', because the first half of one verse runs:

> 'What though the spicy breezes
> Blow soft o'er Ceylon's isle;
> Though every prospect pleases,
> And only man is vile.'

As a little girl I liked little boys, and as a teenager I had no feeling that man was vile. On the contrary, like the lady in the Thurber cartoon, I was delighted that there were two sexes. But vile I'm afraid man is (and woman), as regards wild life.

Britain is not an ideal country for butterflies. It is for the most part grossly overpopulated, the climate is erratic, there are a great number of insect-eating birds either living here or passing through as migrants, our farming methods are extremely efficient, and combined with the urban sprawl this means that waste land is at a premium. Great estates, so important to the preservation of wild life, have been broken up because of heavy taxation. There is considerable industrial pollution, and there are collectors with butterfly nets and dealers in the background.

The common wasp stings caterpillars and chews off the head or tail and feeds on them. The Potter wasp stings them to paralyse them, and then lays its eggs either on or in the caterpillar. When its grubs emerge they feed off their host.

The parasitic wasp.

Many other kinds of wasp, mostly of the Ichneumon family, and also the Tachinid flies are a danger to caterpillars. They inhabit meadows, fields and woodlands. Hundreds of different species are known, and the females of these 'parasitoids' as they are called, all destroy their prey very much in the same peculiarly horrible way as the Potter wasp. They approach the caterpillar and inject their eggs into it. When these eggs hatch, the grubs feed on the fat deposits of the caterpillar, leaving its vital organs intact, so that it wastes away, while yet growing. When the time for pupation arrives, instead of a butterfly, the parasites emerge.

Spiders kill butterflies in various ways. Some catch them in their webs, then bite them, injecting a paralysing fluid, and eat them then and there; others, after injecting them, truss them up and carry them off to be eaten later. Birds, though not quite so lethal, often develop a taste for butterflies, and several species of butterfly have 'eyes' on their wings as a protection, for example the Peacock, the Hedge Brown and the Grayling. The birds tend to go for these 'eyes', and though they may tear the wings, the butterfly itself often escapes as its body has been left intact, and since the 'eyes' are towards the outer edge of the wings, the wings can still be used. It seems ironic that the peacock bird should be very partial to butterflies, but at least peacocks are rare in

Meadow Brown, Grayling and Peacock, showing their 'eyed' markings.
Their enemies: ploughing, boy with net, spider and birds.
(For detailed identification see key on p. 28.)

Britain, unlike pheasants which are reared throughout the country, and often acquire the taste. It seems that not all birds realize that butterflies are good to eat, but that when they find out, other birds copy them.

Weather is of great importance to butterflies. They are predominantly creatures of the sun. Few will fly, feed, mate or lay their eggs unless it is sunny. Rain can do them great harm, especially heavy rain combined with a strong wind. Older butterflies whose wing scales and body hairs are not in prime condition get bedraggled and battered in heavy rain, and so become a prey to predators. Entire colonies are affected by the vagaries of the weather. If, for instance, a period of bad weather happens to coincide with the flight period of a short-lived butterfly, it can have a disastrous effect on numbers, and it may take many years to rebuild the population.

All butterflies avoid rain if they can, though High Brown Fritillaries seem to be able to withstand showers quite well, and often go on feeding after light rain has started; and the dowdy Meadow Browns, whose males have scent scales on their wings to attract the females, will fly up, even during rain, if they are disturbed, only to resettle in long grass further on.[3] Even a cloud will disturb some butterflies. The Common Blue will stop feeding at the approach of a cloud, and clip its wings shut at the approach of rain; so will the Mountain Ringlet; and Brimstones and Orange Tips will find shelter, remaining there motionless, if they become aware, as they almost immediately do, of the presence of cloud. The Wall butterfly (so called because of its habit of basking in the sunshine on walls), Red Admirals, Peacocks, Small Tortoiseshells and Commas all love to sit with wings outstretched on garden paths, giving themselves a sun bath.

Frost can be a killer at the end of October to butterflies that don't hibernate, and in the late spring to young caterpillars. If the food plant has been 'burnt' by frost at this stage, all butterflies in the locality may be exterminated in a single season. Lizards sometimes eat butterflies, and butterflies even get killed on the roads, especially during their airborne courtship when they are oblivious of danger. Earwigs like butterflies' eggs. The robber fly (of which thank goodness there are not many here) attacks butterflies in the air, and takes its prey to a suitable place to suck it dry, and caterpillars are infected by fungal, bacterial and virus diseases.

Lastly we come back to man. Man is dangerous for many reasons. The pesticides he uses have often been suspected of being dangerous to butterflies, and weed killers can also obviously do damage by killing off the food plants of the caterpillars. More serious is the growing habit of spraying old pasture with paraquat in order to kill off all plant life, followed by sod seeding. But most serious of all are the ecological changes man makes, which can upset the habitat of a species and so, since many butterflies are very localized, endanger the existence of a colony.

Modern forestry can produce good conditions in which the Purple Emperor may breed – these occur very extensively through many of the coniferous plantations of West Sussex, Surrey and Hampshire. But on the other hand changed methods of reafforestation have affected several butterflies for the worse. The Forestry Commission are not blameless in this respect. Their commercial policy is frequently in conflict with the conservation of wild life. For instance, weed clearing on a large scale has been carried out; the reduction of brambles makes life harder for the White Admiral and Fritillaries. Also the former needs honeysuckle and the latter violets on which their caterpillars feed. In many places thickets are being destroyed, adversely affecting the Brown Hairstreak.

Some butterflies are becoming very rare, because of such loss or reduction of the food plant of the larvae. In fact the key to the decline of the British butterfly really lies in the understanding of its lifestyle. After all, the butterfly itself only exists in the butterfly form (or 'imago' – plural 'imagines') as the end of a life-cycle which goes from egg to caterpillar to chrysalis to butterfly. It is at its most vulnerable as a caterpillar – normally the longest phase of the cycle, lasting anything from one to six months.

Birds which are enemies to the imago like to eat caterpillars too, and in the spring feed them to their ever-hungry young; but in the final analysis, the caterpillar is so vulnerable because it is so selective in its feeding. The Silver-washed Fritillary lays its eggs on the bark of oak trees, but always in the vicinity of violets, and the caterpillar only lives on violet leaves. If the oaks are felled and the violets are not present, then the Silver-washed Fritillary disappears. The Marsh Fritillary lives only on devil's-bit scabious, which grows only in marshy land. Drain the marsh for agricultural purposes, the devil's-bit scabious vanishes, and so does the Marsh Fritillary.

During the Second World War, probably the most damage was done to our butterfly population. Many thousands of acres of derelict farmland, heathland and permanent pasture were ploughed up in order to grow more food, and they have never been allowed to revert. Luckily, parts of the Dorset Downs are too steep to plough, and the grass here is still close-cropped by sheep and rabbits, so vetches, trefoil and many varieties of grass grow in profusion, and the butterflies that live on them can flourish too. One of them, however, the Adonis Blue, is finding it hard to secure a living elsewhere and is one of our endangered, or at the best very local species.

I can remember as a child seeing butterflies in great numbers in most parts of the country on a sunny day. Now even in a good summer like 1976, it is only certain butterflies in certain areas that dance in such numbers, and the ones that are common are usually the ones whose food plants are also common. The larvae of the Red Admiral, the Small Tortoiseshell (called the Nettle Tortoiseshell in the nineteenth century) and the Peacock live on stinging nettles. The larvae of the Large and Small Whites live on all the cruciferae plants, such as rape, hedge mustard and, of course, cabbages, as well as nasturtium; so do those of the Green-veined White (though their diet doesn't include cabbages). The Hedge Brown caterpillar lives on many types of grass, so does the caterpillar of the Large Skipper; and the Ringlet, the Meadow Brown and the Small Heath live on any grass. The Wall lives on annual meadow grass; the Brimstone on buckthorn; the Orange Tip on charlock, cuckoo flower and garlic mustard; the Speckled Wood on cocksfoot and couch; and the Small Copper on dock and sorrel – all common plants.

One of the invariable lessons nature has taught all down the long ages is that to survive you must, unless you are extraordinarily lucky, be adaptable. Butterflies are no exception.

And to survive, butterflies have found several ways of outwitting their enemies. Some butterflies in a resting position are drab and inconspicuous, but if they see a bird coming towards them, they open their wings suddenly to reveal brilliant colouring. Some adopt uneven ways of flying; others again, like the Brimstones sitting on buckthorn leaves, have a marvellous capacity for camouflage, blending in remarkably well with their surroundings. If Peacocks, which overwinter as butterflies, are disturbed while resting or hibernating, they rub the hairs on their wings together to make a hissing noise. Swallowtails are unpleasant to taste, which seems a good idea, and there is a theory that the Monarch (also known as the Milkweed, a migrant to these shores) is poisonous. Even better! There is also a theory that the Monarch in its native North America is mimicked very closely by another, non-poisonous butterfly (the Viceroy), which in this way gets protection; but on both these points there is controversy. Professor F. A. Urquhart of the University of Toronto, who is one of the world's greatest experts on the Monarch, and has in fact been writing about it since 1911, is doubtful; but the doubters are now very few.[4]

Ringlets, Hedge Browns, Small Whites, Small Heaths and caterpillars, in a hedgerow.
(For detailed identification see key on p. 28.)

However, one thing is irrefutable: many caterpillars are furry or spiny to discourage predators, and many are also masters of camouflage. The Satyridae (the Brown family) live on grass, and their caterpillars are long and thin and pointed at both ends, striped in various shades of green, and so blending with the grass. The Orange Tip caterpillar is also green, and shaded to match the seedpods of its food plant. The Small Copper looks like a small green bump on the leaf on which it feeds, and some of the Hairstreaks lie flat on the under sides of their food plant leaves. The Large Skipper hides itself in a grass tent held together with silk; and so that it won't be detected through its droppings (or 'frass' as they are called) it has found a way of catapulting them, sometimes several inches away! The Heath Fritillary caterpillars are small and black with grey and brown spines, to look like a plantain flower (their food plant); and the caterpillars of the Comma, with their own individual markings, curl on their leaves in such a way that they resemble bird droppings.

Chrysalides also use camouflage to protect themselves. Those of the Black Hairstreak look like bird droppings. The Orange Tip not only looks like the seedpod of its food plant but changes its colour from green to brown in the autumn. The Hesperiidae (the Skippers) roll up, hidden in tubes of grass, and the Satyridae (the Browns) sometimes hang themselves on the plant, remaining green, and sometimes pupate on the ground, forming a loose network of leaves to cover them, almost like a cocoon.

27

Chrysalides have to withstand the rigours of winter, often in fairly exposed conditions, so they have to be strongly joined to their supporting plants, and well able to weather climatic changes. They can survive buried in snow if need be, and can endure temperatures as low as —15° C.

Eggs too can stand an astonishing amount of cold. The eighteenth-century entomologist Boerhaave, who was responsible for publishing much of Swammerdam's work, tried this experiment. I quote: 'I subjected eggs of several insects to a more severe trial than the winter of 1709 [one of the coldest winters ever experienced in Europe]. Among others were those of the Silk Worm and the Elm Butterfly [the Large Tortoiseshell] which I enclosed in a glass vessel, and buried five hours in a mixture of ice and rock salt, when the thermometer fell 6° below zero; notwithstanding which caterpillars were extruded from all the eggs, and exactly at the same time with those which had not been subjected to the experiment. In the succeeding year I exposed them to a still greater degree of cold. I prepared a mixture of rock salt and nitrate of ammonia, and reduced the thermometer to 22° lower than the cold of 1709. They suffered nothing from this rigorous treatment, as they were hatched in due season.'

Kirby and Spence, who published a monograph together in the early nineteenth-century, came to the conclusion that it was impossible to retard the hatching of eggs by cold, but that it was possible to hurry it along with heat. (Spanish women used to hasten the hatching of silkworm eggs by keeping them warm in their bosoms.)

But alas, in spite of all its ingenuity, the butterfly population in Britain is dwindling.

Notes

1. For a comprehensive and erudite description of their enemies, read Chapters 2 and 3 in Volume I of *The Moths and Butterflies of Great Britain and Ireland*, edited by John Heath.
2. Dr Miriam Rothschild, the eminent entomologist, has a tame fox which likes eating butterflies. And during the heat wave and drought of the summer of 1976, rats got into some of the breeding cages at the Worldwide Butterflies farm in Dorset, and devoured every butterfly.
3. Dr Charles Lane found that in Austria, near Gaming, Meadow Browns of the same species as the British ones fly up into the trees if disturbed. (*Entomologist's Monthly*

Magazine, 18 April 1962.)
4. Dr Miriam Rothschild wrote an absorbing article on mimicry in *Natural History* (February 1967), and also, in conjunction with T. Reichstein, J. von Euw and J. A. Parsons, an article called 'Heart Poisons in the Monarch Butterfly' in *Science* (1968, **161**, pp. 861–6). Dr Lincoln Brower and Dr Jane Brower have also done a great deal of research on the subject. All of these entomologists tend to go along with the view that Monarchs are poisonous to their predators, and that the Viceroys mimic them. Professor Urquhart, as can be seen in Appendix 2, has different views on this subject.

Key to illustration on p. 24
1: Meadow Brown (female); 2: Grayling (female); 3: Peacock (female)

Key to illustration on p. 27
1 & 8: Hedge Brown (male); 2: Hedge Brown caterpillar; 3 & 9: Small White (male); 4 & 5: Ringlet (male); 6: Ringlet caterpillar; 7 & 10: Small Heath (female)

3

THE ASTONISHING LIFE HISTORY OF THE LARGE BLUE

Of the species most highly at risk, the Large Blue (*Maculinea arion*) has a life history so extraordinary that the seventeenth-century scientists who scoffed at poor Swammerdam's theory of metamorphosis would have thought the discoverers of it dangerously lunatic. (Incidentally, in view of Swammerdam's great contribution, it is good to see that by 1789 Gilbert White was writing about him with obvious approval in *The Natural History of Selborne*, and also in the late eighteenth century Shaw and Nodder in Volume 5 of *Naturalist's Miscellany* said '. . . and the full persuasion of a "reasoner" like Swammerdam'. In 1832 Captain Thomas Brown was calling him the 'celebrated' Swammerdam in his lovely little book *Brown's Butterflies, etc.*)

The life history of the Large Blue was first described by Captain E. B. Purefoy and F. W. Frohawk, who made their discovery at the time of the First World War. Dr T. A. Chapman made an independent discovery of the life history, as described in Appendix 3.

The egg of the Large Blue is laid singly, and well concealed in the flower head of wild thyme. It hatches in seven to ten days, and for the first three weeks lives a normal caterpillar life, except that it fights and has cannibalistic tendencies if it meets another of its own kind. Otherwise, at this point it is a strict vegetarian, and resembles the thyme blossoms on which it feeds. It changes its skin twice at this stage, and during the second instar (as the stage between moults is called), a honey gland appears. At the third instar, however, a great change occurs. First of all it rests for about six hours, then, showing no further interest in its food plant, it drops to the ground, and waits to be found by an ant (of the genus *Myrmica*). (It will wander away from the thyme, however, if the ground is bare or otherwise unsuitable for ants.)

At this momentous meeting, it is the ant which dominates the proceedings. The caterpillar often appears indifferent, but the ant 'recognizes' it at once, and fondles it with its feet. In response, the caterpillar exudes a tiny drop of sweet liquid from its honey gland, which the ant licks up. This 'milking' may last up to an hour, with the ant leaving periodically, but always returning. Finally the caterpillar takes up a strange attitude. It distends its first three segments, whereupon the ant straddles it, gripping it behind the swollen segments, and takes it to the ant hill, and down to the chambers where the youngest ant grubs are kept. Here it remains in darkness, for the next five or six weeks, feeding on the grubs, with no protests from its hosts, although by this time it doesn't give them any honey! It sleeps through the winter, wakes in the spring, and resumes its carnivorous life. It becomes fully grown without moulting again, and then, still incarcerated in the ants' nest, it hangs itself up by the hindlegs, turns dead white, and in a week's time, pupates.

Silver-spotted Skippers, Chequered Skippers, Heath Fritillaries,
Glanville Fritillary, Purple Emperor, Large Blue and Adonis Blues.
(For detailed identification see key on p. 35.)

The chrysalis falls down, and remains on the ground for about three weeks, until the butterfly emerges. In complete darkness, it then finds its way along the galleries, and out of the nest where it has lived for ten months. Once in the open, it climbs up the stem of a plant, where it remains until its wings have expanded and dried, so that it can fly. It mates and dies within about fifteen or sixteen days.

When it rests by day it faces head downwards, and by night it turns head upwards.

The Large Blue is Britain's rarest butterfly, though the reasons for its decline have not always been clear. While it has had its ups and downs as a species in the past 150 years, its numbers have never before diminished to the extent that they have today.

In the years between 1915 and 1918, Captain Purefoy managed to breed a few. At that time, F. W. Frohawk, one of the world's great entomologists, was attempting to breed every species of British butterfly. The work load was so tremendous that he farmed out the breeding of the Large Blue to Captain Purefoy, who experimented by putting some *Myrmica* ants into a walnut shell, and releasing a caterpillar of the Large Blue. It was 'adopted' by the ants, and so proved that the life-cycle of the Large Blue depended on the intervention of these ants. Purefoy and Frohawk were the first people to breed the Large Blue right through to adults in 1918. Since then several others, including Charles Hulse in 1930, and Professor C. A. Clarke in 1953, have succeeded, but all have followed the walnut method 'like a cookery book' (in Dr Thomas's phrase). As far as is known, all other methods have failed.

In 1963, the Large Blue Committee was formed to study and protect the species.[1] The Committee attempts to manage the butterfly's habitat, and study its needs, and it feels that if enough stock could be produced in captivity, it might be able to restart colonies in some of the butterfly's old localities, or strengthen present ones.

On the Worldwide butterfly farm at Over Compton in Dorset (of which more in Chapter 10), Robert Goodden and his wife Rosemary are investigating a means of producing such captive stocks. With the butterfly on the point of extinction, the question of how to obtain breeding stock was a difficult one, and the need to prepare and keep ants' nests was also a problem. They were about to refuse the Committee's request to make the experiment, when they had the most amazing stroke of luck. They were on holiday in France, and had stopped the car to hunt for Swallowtail caterpillars, when to their astonishment they came across a little colony of Large Blues, on a small bank. They watched the female lay her eggs, and as soon as she had left they collected the eggs, but their problems started immediately. There was no doubt about the butterflies being Large Blues, but their eggs were being laid not on thyme, but on marjoram! They collected the marjoram stems, and brought the eggs and the stems home to England in plastic boxes, but since the find had come about by chance, they were not prepared for the rest of the experiment, and had no idea from where to get the *Myrmica* ants.

Before preparing for the ants, however, they had to provide for the newly hatched caterpillars, and these they put straight on to potted thyme; one caterpillar on each flower head. Within a few days every single caterpillar had disappeared. Fortunately some caterpillars were still hatching, so this time they tried putting each caterpillar into a separate minute plastic box with one floret of thyme. This worked excellently. They still had the old marjoram heads in the original plastic box, and now they were to get another surprise. As these dried out, more and more caterpillars (which had been marvellously well concealed while the plants were still in flower) started to appear, until no less than twenty had proclaimed themselves! These were now all raised in individual boxes, and survived as far as the third instar – the ant stage – with very few losses, so the experiment was under way.

With the help of Dr M. V. Brian, the former Director of the Institute of Terrestrial Ecology's Furzebrook Research Station, a specialist on ants in general and the genus *Myrmica* in particular, they were equipped to start the next stage, and to introduce the ants and caterpillars to one another. It was a disaster. They utterly refused to have anything to do with one another. (Professor

Clarke of Liverpool had found the same thing, twenty years before.) Nothing daunted, the Gooddens put the caterpillars directly into the brood chambers of three ants' nests, but alas, again things didn't happen as they should. They tried varying conditions, and different ants' nests, and eventually a few of the caterpillars were adopted. An adopted caterpillar looks a little hunched up and slightly translucent. Mr Goodden says that it has 'an apparent look of contentment'. At this first attempt, however, the whole stock died in hibernation.

In succeeding years they also got new stocks from abroad, and in the first year there were heavy losses while bringing home the food plant with its eggs and caterpillars, for the food plant either tends to dry up or go mouldy unless the humidity is exactly right. On the second visit they took a motor caravan, especially equipped with a gas refrigerator in which the humidity could be controlled, and they managed to keep the food plants in good condition.

Each year they have learnt more about the requirements of both the Large Blues and the ants. They have found that marjoram is interchangeable with wild thyme, and that it is easier to raise the young caterpillars on the marjoram with the methods they use. They have obtained pairings of the butterflies (the first ever obtained in captivity), and have found it possible to persuade butterflies to lay, quite satisfactorily, and caterpillars have now been reared as far as pupation.

The future of this experiment, as far as the Gooddens are concerned, lies in whether or not funds can be raised to finance it, because the expeditions already undertaken abroad have cost a great deal. If they can, their main object will be to concentrate on persuading the ants to adopt a reasonable number of caterpillars. The Gooddens can now raise the caterpillars up to the ant stage in good numbers, and wish to experiment with several different kinds of ants' nests. They believe that if they can only reduce the large losses at the ant stage, they will have succeeded in finding a viable way to raise a quantity of butterflies, and eventually use British stock to restock British localities.

They also feel that the survival of the Large Blue will almost certainly depend now on the ecological work which has been started by Dr Jeremy Thomas. However, new facts and questions over the life history have come to light through their work on breeding the species at Worldwide Butterflies, and future work may teach us a lot more about the species, both in captivity and in the wild, tying in with the Large Blue's ecological requirements.

Dr Jeremy Thomas started his work on the Large Blue at Monks Wood in 1974. In 1975 he moved to Furzebrook Research Station, which is near Wareham in Dorset; there he spends the winters, and in the summers he goes to the West Country, to the place where the Large Blue still survives. His job is very different from the Gooddens', as he and those with him are not attempting to breed the butterfly in captivity but to manage its habitat and study its requirements so that it can be increased naturally in the wild.

He starts his field work by counting the number of eggs laid. The habitat is divided into different areas, according to the density of the eggs they habitually contain. Counts of eggs are made in every area, but only on a proportion of the thyme plants in each. This proportion varies from searching about one in five plants in the areas with the highest density of eggs, down to about one in twenty of plants in the worst areas. By knowing the number of plants in each area, the proportion searched in each area, and the number of eggs found, it is easy to calculate the total number present on the site to give a fairly truthful picture.

The survival of these (and other) eggs through to adults is then observed, in order to find out at what stage natural mortality occurs, and to see where the main fluctuations occur from year to year. In addition, observations make it possible to compare the survival of eggs to adults in

Large Blues in their habitat, on food plant (wild thyme).
(For male/female identification see key on p. 35.)

different areas of the site which vary very slightly in certain features, such as their aspect, the amount of scrub shading thyme and ants, the height of the grass, the density of thyme, and particularly the species of *Myrmica* that are present. Some areas are also being managed differently to produce more variations, and the survival of the Large Blue is also being studied in these. The outcome has been to discover some conditions that are very good for survival, and the scientists are trying to manage such sites and other areas so that all the ground is in the optimum state, instead of only in the localized patches which occur at present.

All *Myrmica* ants will adopt the Large Blue very readily, but survival is higher in the nests of one particular strain of the ant now known to Furzebrook. They are not taken down to the site from Furzebrook, because they are highly adaptable, and increase very rapidly wherever the habitat is made suitable. The conditions are specialized, but it is proving possible to provide them over far greater areas and on many more sites than hitherto, and this modification of the management has caused a decline in the other species of *Myrmica* in which survival of the Large Blue is poor.

Thyme is taken down to the site because unlike *Myrmica*, its powers of spreading are very slow. It is grown in greenhouses at Furzebrook, and is being introduced to new or improved areas which have already been colonized by *Myrmica*, but which would probably not be available to the Large Blue for perhaps fifty years or more if existing plants were to be left to themselves to spread.

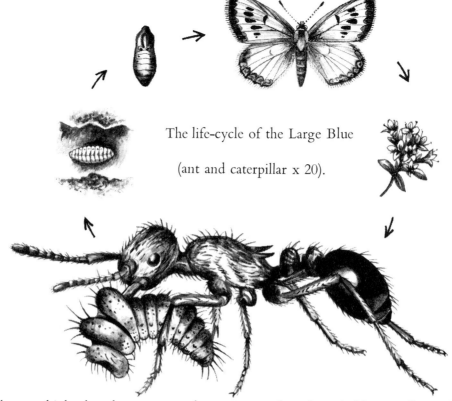

The life-cycle of the Large Blue

(ant and caterpillar x 20).

Dr Thomas thinks that the team now knows some, though probably not all, conditions that are suitable for a Large Blue colony, but unfortunately the knowledge has come perhaps two or three years too late, and he is doubtful whether the butterfly can be saved from extinction. Numbers have declined to such a low level that some luck is also required if a recovery is to occur, even under the best possible conditions.

The Large Blue is now a protected species, and apart from the efforts to reintroduce it, already mentioned, there is also a last-minute attempt to conserve it.

Once it flourished throughout the southern counties and in Devon and Cornwall as well. Now, except for a rare sighting on the Atlantic coast of Cornwall and on the downs near Gloucester, it is making its last stand on a patch of countryside less than a mile square. Not unnaturally the exact location is unpublicized, and naturalists have set up patrols to protect it. Unfortunately, 1977 was a particularly disastrous year for it, perhaps because the summer was exceptionally poor.

The maximum fine for collecting a specimen is £100, enforceable by the Conservation of Wild Creatures and Wild Plants Act of 1975, and it is the only British butterfly ever to have been accorded legal protection.

Up until the early fifties, it was still found in some thirty places, but the loss of its food plant by more efficient farming, plus the fact that myxomatosis has killed off so many of the rabbits whose close cropping of the grass made it easier for the *Myrmica* ants to find the caterpillars, and the use of pesticides, have seen its virtual destruction.

This is Captain Purefoy's own account of his experiment to rear the Large Blue. It is so fascinating that I make no apology for quoting it in its entirety.

'Half an empty walnut shell was placed in a very small, shallow tin box, with a little earth at the bottom. A hole of about 3 mm in diameter was made in the shell near the top. The tin box was stood on a little platform surrounded by water, and into it was introduced a female ant and about twenty workers of *M. laevinodis*, together with a teaspoonful of brood. The ants quickly disappeared under the shell taking the brood with them. In three or four days they were allowed a little more earth, and they were regularly fed. After a week the shell was raised for a brief look, and the brood were seen to be nicely plastered all over the dome of their little home. This was done about the time the first *arion* [Large Blue] ova were hatching.

'The very first *arion* larva to accomplish its third moult was set aside in a box for a few hours to allow the honey gland to develop, and then picked up on a paint brush and invited to walk through the little porthole in the walnut shell straight into the ant brood. This it did, and the hole was closed behind it with a pellet of soil. When 48 hours had elapsed the shell was raised for inspection. There was *arion* on the roof, among the broods, distinctly larger. This larva continued to feed and grow in the nutshell till early October, when he was of ordinary hibernating size. The ant brood was frequently replenished, an eggspoonful of small larvae in their last instar being popped *under* the shell from time to time. As winter approached more soil was added to the box until the shell was just covered, and it was stood in a cold glass house. On Christmas Day the earth was spooned out and the shell lifted. *Arion* and all the ants were hibernating together in the shell. They were buried again without being in the least disturbed. About the middle of April the shell was again examined. Activity had been resumed and some more brood added. The larva finally pupated in the shell, fixed at first to the roof by the cremaster, but later it lay on the soil with the ants constantly moving over it. A bit of net was tied over the top of the tin box, and one morning three weeks later a fine male imago was found hanging to the net. The ant passages under the shell through the soil on which it lay were evidently quite sufficient for it to effect its escape!'

Incidentally, Captain Purefoy was Rosemary Goodden's grandfather.

Notes

1. Alan Kennard, M.B.E., is the Secretary. He is the only man to be honoured for his work on butterflies, and before the Large Blue Committee was formed, he did a great deal of work on his own to try to conserve the butterfly.

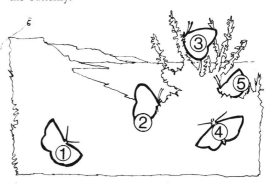

Key to illustration on p. 30
1: Purple Emperor (male); 2 & 3: Silver-spotted Skipper (male); 4: Glanville Fritillary (male); 5 & 11: Adonis Blue (male); 6 & 7: Chequered Skipper (male); 8: Large Blue (female); 9 & 10: Heath Fritillary (male)
Key to illustration on p. 33
1 & 5: Large Blue (female); 2, 3 & 4: Large Blue (male)

4

ATTEMPTS TO REINTRODUCE THE SWALLOWTAIL AND THE LARGE COPPER

The Swallowtail

The British form of Swallowtail butterfly (*Papilio machaon britannicus*) is not the kind that Maria Merian would have painted and described so lovingly. It differs from the Continental forms in colour, in its sort of habitat, and in its food plant. Here, it now only resides in fenland around the Norfolk Broads, and restricts itself to milk parsley.

At one time it occurred throughout the East Anglian fens, and in the marshes of the Thames and Lea Rivers. (Moses Harris in the eighteenth century said that he found one in 'the meadows' of Bristol.) During the seventeenth, eighteenth and nineteenth centuries, these fens and marshes were drained for agricultural purposes. By 1850, the work was finished. So also, in these places, was the butterfly.

Outside Norfolk, it was only at Wicken Fen, one of the last remaining fragments of the once large areas of Cambridgeshire fen, that the species held out, until the early 1950s. Then it died. Repeated attempts to re-establish it from laboratory stock taken from Norfolk failed. Why it died out then, and why the experiments to reintroduce it have failed, remain as yet a mystery.

The butterfly is on the wing from late May until mid-July. The males are territorial, and centre their activities round a single large bush or tree, from which they make warning forays against other males. The females usually lay their eggs on milk parsley, and generally on those parts of the plant which stand above the surrounding vegetation. The eggs, which are large and conspicuous, are pale yellow at first. Soon they darken to brown, then plum colour, then black. They hatch in about two weeks, and the caterpillars, which are black with a broad white band, look like bird droppings. They begin life by eating their own eggshells before starting on the food plant. They are solitary, moult four times, and last as caterpillars for about a month. When disturbed, they erect a bright orange osmeterium (a pair of retractible tubercles in the shape of a V which when erected reveals a small slit) from behind their heads, and emit a pungent smell like a pineapple. After the second moult they change utterly in appearance, becoming bright green with black and orange spotted rings, and at this stage they move to the top of the plant to feed on the developing flower heads. By the end of July they are fully grown, and leave the plant to pupate on reed or sedge, or sometimes on the lower twigs of bushes. The pupa is fastened head upwards to a reed or its food plant by its tail-hooks and a silken girdle. Most pupae go through the winter and emerge as butterflies the following summer, but in some years a few Swallowtails emerge after a three-week pupation in August, and produce a second lot of eggs.

The habitat and life-cycle of the Swallowtail, on food plant (milk parsley).
(For detailed identification see key on p. 41.)

Although the butterfly is declining as a species, egg mortality is low. No egg parasites appear to attack them, and what mortality occurs seems to be the result of infertility, usually in years when the weather has been bad, and mating has been restricted.

In the first two instars of the caterpillar, mortality is high, mainly through the depredations of spiders. By the third instar, the caterpillars are too big for spiders, and seem to be fairly safe, but during the fourth and early fifth instars, they become a prey to birds. At Hickling Broad in Norfolk, bird predation is heavy, but at Woodbastwick it is considerably less, perhaps because there are far fewer caterpillars and the local birds haven't yet acquired the taste. At Wicken, although reed warblers and sedge warblers were there in abundance during the efforts at reintroduction, they took no caterpillars at all, but then at Wicken the numbers were very small indeed.

The pupae suffer from predation by small mammals.

Although the Swallowtail population at Wicken died out just over twenty years ago, it had persisted there before then, in isolation, for more than two hundred years. It isn't known whether this long period in isolation affected the insect biologically, but it is clearly more than possible. For instance, there are signs that during the 1880s the Wicken butterflies opted for less mobility; perhaps because of the small size of their available habitat. If this is so, it must at least have some bearing on the difficulties of introducing stock from Norfolk into Wicken. There were also changes to the Norfolk butterflies around 1920 to 1930. For instance, the width of the thorax – the division of an insect's body that bears the legs and wings – had decreased to equal that of the Wicken butterflies. Yet it doesn't seem that any of these changes should have made the chance of establishing the Norfolk butterflies at Wicken impossible, so why the failure?

Wicken Fen has gradually become drier since the drainage of the East Anglian Fens, which led to its isolation. Also with the drainage of the surrounding land, the water table has lowered, and that, with the oxidation and shrinkage of the peat soils, has had the effect that the fen is now between two and three metres higher than the rest of the land. This has led to its invasion by woody plants. The amount of open fen vegetation has been much reduced, and milk parsley, which is usually found in sedge and litter fields, can now only be maintained by repeated burning and mowing, to prevent the growth of carr. (Carr is the name for the bush thickets that like damp ground – such as alder-buckthorn, sallow, and guelder rose.) The Second World War played its part here, too. Because of the reduction in the use of sedge and reed for thatching during the war, cutting was abolished, and this may have been the final death knell for the Swallowtail at Wicken. By the time the butterfly had become extinct, its suitable habitat had decreased from over 121.5 hectares to 8.1 (i.e. 300 acres to 20).

During the past fifteen years, the sedge and litter fields there have been deliberately increased threefold, for the benefit of the Swallowtail, but the distribution of milk parsley is still extremely patchy, and the plants at Wicken are smaller, produce less seed, and are shorter-lived than those on the Broads.

Dr J. P. Dempster and Mrs M. L. King from the Institute of Terrestrial Ecology's Monks Wood Experimental Station in Huntingdonshire, and Mr K. H. Lakhani from the Institute of Terrestrial Ecology at Cambridge, have written a fascinating and detailed paper on all this, called 'The Status of the Swallowtail Butterfly in Britain', published in 1976; they conclude that the main requirements for the success of introducing the Norfolk breed of Swallowtail to Wicken is a more generous growth of *Peucedanum* (milk parsley) plants, and that the best way to achieve this would be to reduce the height of the land's surface by peat cutting. This, after all, is the way the Broads were originally made. There is the possibility that if they do succeed, bird predation may become more prevalent, but not more so than in Norfolk.

On the Broads, the Swallowtail seems to be holding its own fairly well, and can be found by the Bure, Yare, Thurne and Ant watercourses. It breeds chiefly round the Hickling and Ranworth Broads, and Horsey Mere.

The Large Copper

It is likely that the Large Copper (*Lycaena dispar dispar* Haw.) became extinct in this country in the early 1850s. There is a record of one being caught in 1851, in Bottisham Fen. Before that, the last specimens had been captured in 1847 or 1848 in Holme Fen, in Huntingdonshire. The first mention of the butterfly was in 1795, and it was described as being very beautiful and very local. Unfortunately its beauty probably led to its extinction, by over-collecting.

In his *Butterflies and Moths of the Countryside*, F. Edward Hulme (1841–1909) says that Haworth (a well-known entomologist[1]) collected sixty in one day in 1827. (It is ironic that such a predator should be commemorated in the 'Haw.' of the butterfly's Latin name!) Hulme also says that people were so greedy that one man claimed to have captured 'sixteen to the half hour', and that

The habitat and life-cycle of the Large Copper at Woodwalton Fen.
(For detailed identification see key on p. 41.)

Butterfly eggs, much enlarged. Far left: Large White (x 36); top, left to right: Chalk Hill Blue (x 42) and Essex Skipper (x 30); bottom, left to right: Large Copper (x 36) and Swallowtail (x 36).

Large Copper butterflies could be sold locally for two shillings a dozen 'if one took them as they came', but two-and-six a dozen 'if selected'. In 1902, however, nine specimens fetched a total of £44.6s. at auction.

The butterfly's main locality was in the fen area round Whittlesea Mere (now called Whittlesey), reaching to Yaxley and Holme fens.

Whittlesey Mere, the most famous of the natural lakes in lowland Britain, covered an area of 400–600 hectares (about 1,000–1,500 acres), depending on the tidal level of the River Nene. The reeds round the Mere covered about eighty hectares (nearly 200 acres), and there were large tracts of unreclaimed land to the south and south-east, where plants characteristic of acid bog peat flourished. Here the Large Copper was so abundant in the 1820s that it is almost impossible to believe that thirty years later it would have become extinct.

The first attempt to reintroduce it into Britain was made in 1909, when G. H. Verrall liberated a number of larvae of *Lycaena dispar rutilus* (a European subspecies) on Wicken Fen. It didn't survive, and the theory is that its food plant, the great water dock, was too scarce. In 1913, Captain Purefoy established the first successful colony of these butterflies, at Greenfields, Tipperary, in Eire, in a small bog which had been specially planted with great water dock. In May of that year 120 larvae taken from the marshes north of Berlin were liberated at Greenfields, and in the following summer about 400 butterflies obtained from the same German locality were also released. This colony survived until 1936.

However, in 1915, a Dutch race of Large Copper was found, which enormously excited entomologists, as it was almost indistinguishable from the extinct British race. This was *Lycaena dispar batavus*. The Committee for the Protection of British Lepidoptera, which had been founded by W. G. Sheldon in 1925, and of which Lord Rothschild was Chairman (see Appendix 4), decided to try and introduce some of these to Woodwalton Fen, which was owned by the Hon. Charles Rothschild (see Appendix 5). Late in 1926 they cleared part of the Fen of bushes, and quantities of great water dock were planted. In 1927 twenty-five males and thirteen females were released here, and ever since the cleared area has been called the 'Copper Field'.[2]

In 1963, control of Woodwalton Fen was transferred to the Nature Conservancy at Monks Wood Experimental Station where the Large Copper became the responsibility of Dr Eric Duffey. The Woodwalton Fen Advisory Committee gave the butterfly breeder, Mr E. G. Short of Esher in Surrey, some Large Copper stock in 1960, on the understanding that he would return part of it if necessary. He agreed, so extinction has for the moment been averted. However, Dr Duffey's sad conclusion is that the Large Copper at Woodwalton is unlikely to survive permanently under natural conditions, because the Fen is too small, and the population unaided could probably never withstand the combined assault of predators, parasites and adverse climatic conditions.

Dr Duffey's paper dealing with this, published in 1968 in the *Journal of Applied Ecology* (vol. 5, pp. 69–96), is definitive, and he and Mr Gordon Mason, who is responsible for the field work at Woodwalton, have more first-hand knowledge about the subject than anyone else.

In 1926 the German subspecies was introduced to the Norfolk Broads, but it failed within two years because its food plant didn't grow in the open marshland, where the females like to lay their eggs. The Dutch race at Woodwalton, however, has been maintained ever since its introduction.

Two batches of the Dutch Large Copper were liberated on Wicken Fen, the first in 1930 and the second in either 1931 or 1932. They did very well, and unlike those at Woodwalton never needed to be artificially maintained by rearing larvae in cages. In the late 1930s they were still going strong at Adventurers Fen (a part of Wicken), but in 1942 Adventurers Fen was reclaimed for agriculture, and they disappeared. In 1949 eighty butterflies were liberated in the Yare valley, on the Norfolk Broads near Surlingham, where they flourished until 1951 when exceptionally high tides occurring at just the time the larvae were coming out of hibernation drowned them. Birds also were greedy predators by this time, having acquired a taste for them. Whitethroats developed the unpleasant habit of pursuing them in the evening, devouring the bodies, and discarding the wings.

In *Brown's Butterflies, etc*, Captain Brown mentions that in 1833 the Large Copper was then 'not uncommon in Scotland'. Its occurrence there, however, is highly improbable.

Notes

1. Haworth never believed in the migration of butterflies. In 1830 he wrote, 'To suppose they come over from the continent is an idle suggestion.'
2. James Stuart, who was in the service of Charles Rothschild, managed the Fen for twenty-five years, until he retired in 1937. (He asked that his ashes should be scattered in the woodland at Ashton Wold, owned by Miriam Rothschild.) He was succeeded by George Mason, a Woodwalton man who had been employed as 'Watcher under Stuart' in 1924 and was keeper for thirty-one years; his son, Gordon Mason, is now the manager.

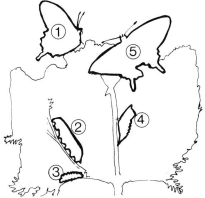

Key to illustration on p. 37
1 & 5: Swallowtail (female); 2: Final instar of Swallowtail caterpillar; 3: First instar of Swallowtail caterpillar; 4: Swallowtail pupa

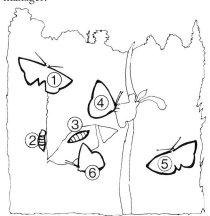

Key to illustration on p. 39
1 & 4: Large Copper (female); 2: Large Copper pupa; 3: Large Copper caterpillar; 5 & 6: Large Copper (male)

5

AN ENDANGERED SIX –
AND THE PURPLE EMPEROR

Chequered Skippers (top and centre: male; bottom: female) and caterpillar on food plants (ground ivy and slender false brome).

When I asked John Heath, the entomologist in charge of insect distribution mapping in the Biological Records Centre at Monks Wood Experimental Station, which butterflies he felt were most endangered, he suggested the Large Blue, the Chequered Skipper, the Heath Fritillary, the Glanville Fritillary, the Silver-spotted Skipper and the Adonis Blue. Some naturalists also consider that the Purple Emperor is in danger, so I will include it here; but since the Large Blue was the subject of Chapter 3, I will not refer to it in this one.

The **Chequered Skipper** (*Carterocephalus palaemon*) is an enchanting little woodland butterfly, which used sometimes to be seen flying along sunny rides in Rutland, Lincolnshire, Huntingdonshire and Northamptonshire. In 1939, a colony was also discovered in Western Inverness.

Next to the Lulworth Skipper, it is one of our most local butterflies. The males and females are almost identical. They are very difficult to spot because they move in short and extremely swift darting movements from flower to flower of the bugle. They are darkish on the upper surfaces, and the under surfaces are dappled yellow; they match their surroundings astonishingly well. The clubs of the antennae are almost pointed.

The eggs are laid singly on blades of grass, and hatch within ten days. The larvae have the extraordinary habit of eating only the edges of the centre stretch of the grass blade, then fastening the edges of what remains with a few strands of silk, which shrink and so form a tube. They then feed on the grass both above and below the tube until virtually only their tube is left on the midrib, when they move to another blade and repeat the process. They are solitary, and feed by night. By mid-October, after the fourth and last moult, they make a large tube, called a hibernaculum, in which they hibernate until March. After this period they cease to feed, and in early April they spin three blades of grass together to make a tent, in which the pupae stand, held by a silken belt, for about six weeks. After this, the butterfly emerges, and lives for about a month. It is so like the Duke of Burgundy Fritillary that only the practised eye can tell them apart at a glance.

Miss Lynne Farrell of Monks Wood is an expert on the Chequered Skipper, and she says it is in danger because of habitat changes. Several areas where it used to flourish have been clear-felled and replanted with conifers. Open rides with their abundance of flowering plants have become overgrown, and climatically a series of dry springs has also contributed to their decline.

Dr Miriam Rothschild, the entomologist and great flea expert, says that during extensive tree felling at Ashton Wold, where she lives, she observed that the Chequered Skippers actually moved away from the denser portions into grassy clearings in the vicinity of unfelled trees.

The **Heath Fritillary** (*Mellicta athalia*) is, unexpectedly, essentially a creature of the woodlands, though it inhabits open country such as heaths where timber and undergrowth have recently been cleared. It is extremely local, and is disappearing fast. Formerly rather widespread in the south of England, the species is now found only in Blean Woods, near Canterbury in Kent, and a few places in Devon and Cornwall.

Like the Chequered Skipper, the males of the Heath Fritillary are difficult to tell apart from the females, though, also like the Chequered Skipper, the females are a little larger and paler. The Heath Fritillary resembles the Glanville Fritillary fairly closely. In both the sexes markings on the forewings read 08:80, and unlike other Fritillaries the species bears neither silver nor black spots on the under side of its wings.

The eggs (about three hundred in number) are laid in sprawling batches, usually under the leaves of ribwort plantain, but occasionally on cow-wheat, and they hatch in about sixteen days. The gregarious larvae remain among the eggshells for some days after hatching, and then spin webs under the leaves and begin to feed on various parts of the plant. The caterpillars go out in small parties to feed, but return to the rest of the brood between times. After the third moult they hibernate under a protective silken web, or inside a curled leaf, and when hibernation is over they often shelter under dead leaves. They moult a further three times and feed only in sunlight. When frightened, the caterpillars display the curious habit of throwing up their heads in joint alarm. The pupae, hanging from their tail-hooks, last about fifteen days.

Heath Fritillaries (top and centre: female; bottom: male) on narrow-leafed plantain.

The butterflies are slow on the wing, but very graceful as they skim from flower to flower of the cow-wheat, bugle, thistle, bell-heather and ragged robin. They have an odd way of perching with their forewings laid back between the hindwings, and have been known to lie doggo, pretending to be dead, when caught. There is only one generation a year, and hibernation always takes place in the larval stage.

A survey of the Heath Fritillary in the West Country was carried out by Dr Robert M. Pyle, a young American, as a part of his Fulbright Scholarship studies in butterfly conservation under the supervision of John Heath at Monks Wood in 1972. Dr Pyle founded the Xerces Society, the insect habitat conservation group, and he is the Chairman of the Lepidoptera Specialist Group of the Survival Service Commission of I.U.C.N. (the International Union for the Conservation of Nature[1]). He found the Heath Fritillary absent from most of the old locations where previously it had thrived. He believes that the distribution of the Heath Fritillary depends very much on the history of disturbance of its habitats. Coppicing (making a wood of small growth for periodic cutting) as a form of woodland management seems to produce the right conditions in Kent. Here, the coppice is chestnut, and the cycle roughly twelve (eight to fifteen) years; quite a short period. For a change, here is a butterfly which needs disruption of its habitat rather than being left alone. The problem is, what kind of disturbance to apply, when, and exactly where. The late Enid Campbell (1916–74) seemed to have the right formula for the site she managed on behalf of the Cornish Naturalists' Trust. Dr Pyle thinks that the Heath Fritillary's chances are good in England, if we can learn a good deal more about its needs, but time is short.

The Reverend A. H. H. (Anthony) Harbottle, an amateur breeder of repute, believes with other lepidopterists that the West Country type of Heath Fritillary only lives on ribwort plantain, but that the 'Kent' population prefers cow-wheat. He also points out that the West Country form differs in appearance.

The **Glanville Fritillary** (*Melitaea cinxia*) is an extremely localized butterfly, occurring only in the Isle of Wight, though it used once to occur on the mainland of England in a few southern localities. It takes its name from a Lady Glanville who lived mostly in the seventeenth century, and who, like poor Swammerdam, was considered to be highly eccentric because she had such a passionate interest in butterflies.

Moses Harris tells us in *The Aurelian*, when describing the Glanville (or 'Plantain Fritillary' as it was sometimes called): 'This fly took its name from the ingenious Lady Glanville, whose memory had nearly suffered for her curiosity. Some relations that were disappointed by her Will, attempted to set it aside by acts of lunacy, for they suggested that none but those who were deprived of their senses would go in pursuit of Butterflies. Her relations and legatees cited Sir Hans Sloane[2] [of Hans Place and Sloane Square fame] in support of their case but fortunately a Mr Rae defended her character. This last gentleman went to Exeter, and on the trial satisfied the judge and jury of the lady's laudable inquiry into the wonderful works of Creation, and established her Will.' (In Appendix 6 there is a list of references to Lady Glanville in various publications.)

The Glanville Fritillary is in danger of disappearing for the same reason as the others – the loss of habitat. It likes steep, untilled slopes, usually near the sea, and due to a combination of cultivation and cliff erosion, many of its favoured sites have been destroyed. It is, however, a very puzzling butterfly, as its colonies have waxed and waned over the years. It has given great cause for alarm from time to time, but it seems to have been more successful just recently.

Glanville Fritillaries (top right: male; others: female) on food plant (sea plantain)
in the Isle of Wight, showing eroded cliff edge.

In 1909 it was in a very bad way, but then became established along the coast from Luccombe
to Chale, and on Boniface Down. It had good years in 1945 and 1949. Another very good year
was 1953, when butterflies covered much of the island, even away from the undercliff. So was
1971, but according to the amateur entomologist T. D. Fearnehough, who lives in the Isle of
Wight, by 1972 the species had retracted again, and all the inland colonies and many of the
coastal ones had disappeared. He claims that many of the inland colonies were, in fact, 'introduc-
tions', made by the release of surplus insects, bred by entomologists.

In 1977 Dr M. G. Morris, the Senior Officer at Furzebrook, reported that the caterpillars of
the Glanville Fritillary were very abundant in the Ventnor undercliff.

The eggs are laid in large batches of between two hundred to three hundred, on plantain
leaves, and they hatch in about twenty days. The larvae are gregarious and live under a silken
web until they hibernate, when they weave a silk nest with internal partitions, and an entrance
hole underneath. After hibernation they don't bother any more about silk coverings, and feed
together, but stay absolutely motionless when there is no sun, or even during cloud. They become
chrysalides after the sixth moult and choose plant stems or the under sides of upright stones to
hang themselves from. They emerge as butterflies in about twenty days.

Unless frightened, the butterflies have a slow and graceful flight, and they keep low to the ground. They choose mostly yellow plants to feed on: hawkweed, crosswort, bird's-foot trefoil, horseshoe vetch and, most often of all, kidney vetch. They also like restharrow, which is pink. As in the case of the Heath Fritillary, the males bask with their forewings laid back over their hindwings. They live as butterflies for about twenty-five days. On their forewings there are markings which resemble OB ꓭO.

Even before they became an endangered species, some people think they were rare, as they prefer a warm climate, and the Isle of Wight is the furthest north they care to venture.

The **Silver-spotted Skipper** (*Hesperia comma*) was locally common in England until the last war. Now it can only be seen very rarely in its habitat of chalk and limestone, in counties south of the Thames, and in Hertfordshire and Buckinghamshire.

Besides being an endangered species, it is also very hard to see, as it only chooses places where the chalk is showing through the surface of the soil, and fescue grass is growing. Here it often flies in company with the Chalk Hill Blue, but it flies rapidly in a darting movement, and settles frequently, with its wings closed. The pure white spots on the under sides of its wings make it easy to distinguish from any other Skipper. (Albinos have been found, and in their case the long scent scale marks on the forewings of the males turn to a dull lilac.)

It hibernates as an egg for seven months, and there is only one generation a year. The eggs are laid singly on blades of fescue grass, and occasionally, some claim, on bird's-foot trefoil, and the caterpillars emerge at the end of March, or early in May. The lifespan of the caterpillar is around a hundred days, and as soon as it hatches from the egg by a small round hole, it makes itself a tent by joining several blades of grass together with silk. It remains there in seclusion, and hidden, and feeds at night. If touched, it crawls backwards very quickly and hides deeper in the grass.

After the fourth moult, which is its last, it makes a strong cocoon of silk and pieces of grass and grass stems, which it has bitten off, not far from the ground, and pupates. The pupa attaches itself to the cocoon by means of numerous hooks, and emergence occurs in about ten days.

The butterfly flies very low and very fast, and unlike most Skippers, when it rests it chooses short turf, bare ground and sheep's droppings in preference to bushes, leaves and tall vegetation, though it does sometimes feed on thistles, knapweed and yellow hawksbit. When it sunbathes, its forewings are slightly open, and its hindwings open completely. In this position it looks rather like a moth. At night, however, it rests as other

Silver-spotted Skippers on food plant (sheep's fescue).
(For male/female identification see key on p. 51.)

butterflies do, with its wings closed. Its lifespan as a butterfly is only fifteen or sixteen days. ·

It has become so rare because it likes steep slopes where the grasses are close-cropped by rabbits, and myxomatosis has taken a toll of the rabbits. However, in 1977 a new locality was found in Dorset, where the butterfly seems to be flourishing.

The male of the **Adonis Blue** (*Lysandra bellargus*) is usually a brilliant, very pure blue, though its colour and markings may be subject to drastic aberrations. The female is dark brown, probably for camouflage when she lays her eggs. The butterflies are very vivacious and gregarious, living in colonies, and they fly swiftly, with a fluttering, rather erratic flight. In the eighteenth century, butterflies were described as 'living in societies'. (Is this the reason for the phrase 'a social butterfly'?[3]) They pause often to feed from wild flowers, and both sexes bask with their wings only half open, on the heads of flowers. In courtship, several males pursue one female, and the one that reaches her first is the accepted suitor. They live on chalk and limestone downs, and hills, along the south coast of England. They are double-brooded, and hibernate as larvae.

Adonis Blues on food plant (horseshoe vetch) in grazing land, with typical flora and fauna.
(For male/female identification see key on p. 51.)

The eggs are laid singly on horseshoe vetch, usually on the under side of the leaves, and, depending on the temperature, they hatch in eighteen to as many as forty days, according to Edmund Sandars, in his *Butterfly Book for the Pocket*. When the larvae appear, they feed only on horseshoe vetch, and at night. During the day they hide.

The larvae from the May to June eggs produce imagines in August and September; the eggs from these imagines produce larvae which overwinter but do not feed up until the spring. These larvae spin a layer of silk from a mass of silken threads, and hibernate under a leaf of their food plant. The larvae feed in the early evening. The Adonis Blue larvae also have an association with *Myrmica* ants; the larvae are often smothered with them, and probably gain some protection from predators in this way.

There are four moults, and when it is about to pupate the larva hides itself, sometimes on the surface of the ground under the plant among dried grass, usually making a little cocoon, and sometimes actually burrowing into soft ground to a depth of about half an inch. The pupa lasts for about twenty days.

The Adonis Blue was becoming very rare because of the changing grazing pattern on the downs, and partly too because of fluctuation in climate and weather. As with other downland butterflies, the agricultural changes during the last war were responsible in large measure for their decline, but just recently they seem to have made something of a comeback, and could perhaps be put on a list of very local species, rather than endangered. Let's hope so, though 1977, again, was a particularly bad year.

The **Purple Emperor** (*Apatura iris*), certainly one of our most magnificent and beautiful indigenous butterflies, has as I have said been considered by some to be endangered.[4] Although it has often been considered to be very scarce, it had good years in 1868, 1881, 1905 and 1911, when it was fairly common, and it is probably more widespread today than is generally appreciated. The males and females are very different, not only in appearance (the male being the only one to have the purple sheen on its wings – the iridescence being produced by the structure of the wing scales) but also in their habits.

Female Purple Emperor on sallow.

Purple Emperors (male) in their habitat at the top of oak trees.

Their habitat is restricted to woodlands – chiefly tall oaks – in the south of England, mostly in Surrey, Sussex and Hampshire, and they live as butterflies from four to five weeks.

The males are rarely seen, not only because they are few, but because they prefer to stay in the highest branches of tall trees, unless lured to ground level by something either white or glittering, or to feed on decaying animal juices, or on the moisture from middens. However, recent evidence suggests that they are turning vegetarian, preferring sap and puddles to their former diet. They are extremely territorial, choosing favourite boughs on which to sit. In wet weather they shelter on tree trunks. They seldom visit flowers of any kind. From their vantage point so high up, they display a lively interest in everything that happens around them.

The drabber females on the other hand make frequent descents, and only visit high trees for pairing. They fly low over the ground.

Both sexes have a majestic imperial flight. They soar and glide across glades in the woodland, swiftly and strongly, and they show their inquisitiveness by flying and swooping almost directly at anybody who happens to come nearby, as though they want to inspect him.

The female lays her eggs singly on the upper side of a sallow leaf, near the edge, and according to Frohawk almost always on the right-hand side! The eggs hatch in about fourteen days, and the larva eats its way out of the top of the shell. Once out, it eats the rest of the shell. It then spins a web and settles down on the midrib of the leaf, feeding by day. After its first moult, which occurs in three days, horns appear on its head. After the second moult, when it is still quite small, it spins another web, on which it stretches itself out straight, to look like a bud. The web is usually spun in a fork. It hibernates like this until the buds begin to burst in the spring, its colour changing with the colour of its home. When the caterpillar is crawling, it cocks its horns stiffly, and when it is resting, it lays them forward. If touched it whirls the front half of its body towards the intruder, as if to toss it with its horns, and if disturbed in any other way, it wriggles the front half of its body quickly, from side to side. When fully grown its web takes up a whole leaf, and it goes to other leaves to feed, but returns to its web to rest.

After four moults it is ready to pupate, and it spins silk down the leaf rib, and secures this to the stem so that the leaf won't fall while it is in hibernation. It then lies for two days with its head towards the stalk of the leaf, and then two days facing the tip of the leaf, after which it pupates, with the chrysalis hanging from numerous small tail-hooks. The chrysalis, which is green, has two horns, and lasts for about fourteen days.

In the nineteenth century the Purple Emperor was known as 'Emperor of the Woods', or the 'Purple Highflier Butterfly'.

As I have mentioned the 'wing scales' of the Purple Emperor, perhaps Dr Johnson's description of them might be appropriate: 'That which seems to be a powder on the wings of a butterfly is an innumerable company of extreme small feathers'!

Eleazar Albin had this to say: '. . . the Colours, particularly of the Moths and Butterflies (which to our Eyes seem as Dust), if they be examined by a *Microscope*, every *Particle* of them is a perfect Feather, and is placed in the Wing in most exact Order.'

Notes

1. The I.U.C.N., whose President is Sir Peter Scott, is compiling a red data book on species which are endangered.

2. Sir Hans Sloane's daughter married Charles, (later) the 2nd Baron Cadogan, and commemorated her father on the Cadogan property in London.

Eleazar Albin, in his Introduction to *A Natural History of English Insects*, wrote: 'For this curious lady [a Mrs How, his patroness], Widow of the late Physician of that Name, I painted a great Number of both *Caterpillars* and *Flies* [by flies he meant butterflies and moths] and likewise several things relating to Natural History for Sir *Hans Sloane*.' More importantly, Sir Hans Sloane's collection was the basis of that at the Natural History Museum.

3. Mary Russell Mitford, writing in a letter about Jane Austen, described her as the 'prettiest, silliest, most affected, husband-hunting butterfly' she ever remembered! (In later years she described her as 'perpendicular, precise and taciturn'.)

J. J. Joicey (1871–1932), whose large and valuable collection of butterflies is now at the British Museum (Natural History), was encouraged by his mother to start collecting them, in the hope that it would deflect him from chasing the human variety all the time!

4. Dr Morris and Dr Thomas of Furzebrook don't agree that the Purple Emperor is endangered; while acknowledging that it is extremely scarce in Huntingdonshire and Norfolk, they feel that it is quite widespread in Oxfordshire and Buckinghamshire.

The fact that very distinguished entomologists sometimes disagree with each other is one of the fascinations the study of butterflies has for me. It is by no means yet a finite subject.

Key to illustration on p. 46
1, 3 & 4: Silver-spotted Skipper (male)
2 & 5: Silver-spotted Skipper (female)

Key to illustration on p. 47
1, 2 & 4: Adonis Blue (male)
3 & 5: Adonis Blue (female)

OTHER RARE INDIGENOUS BUTTERFLIES

In Dickens's *Bleak House*, Harold Skimpole says, 'I only ask to be free. The butterflies are free.' But as we have seen, the freedom of a butterfly is relative. The threats to their habitat, and their many enemies, have put at risk more than those on John Heath's list of endangered species, and in some cases have finished off the species here entirely.

The **Black-veined White** (*Aporia crataegi*) is accepted as being extinct in Britain. As Dr Morris says, 'It is always impossible to prove a negative, but we can be reasonably certain that it has been extinct for some decades.' In the nineteenth century it was widespread in southern England and Wales, but it gradually began to decline until in 1925 it was found only in Kent. There is a school of thought which believes that a tiny colony still inhabits an area in Kent, but the opponents of this belief think some captive-bred butterflies are released there occasionally for collectors.

Black-veined Whites on blackthorn.

Both males and females are alike to look at, but the wings of the females are semi-transparent as the wing scales are very thin. The butterflies are white, with heavy black veining. They overwinter gregariously as caterpillars in a thick silk web, spun in the fork of a plum or apple tree, or on hawthorn or blackthorn bushes. When they waken in the spring, the little hairy caterpillars bask on their web before feeding on the new green shoots of their food plant. Starting at the top, they move down it backwards, eating as they go. If disturbed, they either crawl away very rapidly into the thick part of the tree or bush, returning only when all danger seems to be past, or they quickly let themselves down from the food plant on a thin silken thread, and then crawl away on the ground. When fully grown they are a tawny brown with fairer hairs sprouting out of white warts. Along the sides and back there are black stripes. During the final instar they become solitary, spinning a silk pad, and attaching themselves by a silken girdle to a thick branch, before turning into chrysalides.

It has been suggested that climatic conditions, bringing moister weather which could have spread virus diseases to the larvae, may have been responsible for their sudden decline. Also a tiny parasitic wasp, *Apanteles glomeratus*, attacks the larvae of the Black-veined White. (Edmund Sandars says, '*Apanteles glomeratus* may be translated as "massed imperfection"!')

The **Mountain Ringlet** (*Erebia epiphron*) is very local in England, occurring only in the Lake District. It is more plentiful in the Highlands of Perthshire and Inverness, particularly at heights above 1,500 feet. The Scottish form is slightly larger than the English.

There is a theory that it could have come here during the latter part of the Pleistocene glaciation, and that it is one of the three Alpine butterflies which reached here in glacial times and spread northwards as the ice cap receded. The lifespan of the butterfly is about twenty days.

The eggs are laid singly on mat grass, and hatch in eighteen to twenty days. The newly arrived caterpillars eat their eggshells, then continue by eating their food plant, for about two months, until half grown. They then crawl into a grass tussock and go into hibernation. In the spring they waken, and feed from the shoots that have sprouted after the snows have melted away. When the time comes for them to pupate they burrow among the grass, and draw a few random blades together with silk.

The butterflies are brown with several eyes along both the forewings and the hindwings. Their flight is fast, low and fluttering. They will only fly in the sunshine, disappearing into the grass at the first hint of cloud – which, considering that their

Mountain Ringlets (top and bottom: male; centre: female) on mat grass in their habitat.

53

habitat is so often obscured in mist, seems odd. Furthermore, since they only mate in sunshine, and the weather where they live is very uncertain, not to mention the fact that their lifespan is so short, it is wonderful they are still with us and manage to flourish, if only locally.

The **Large Tortoiseshell** (*Nymphalis polychloros*), unlike the Small Tortoiseshell, is rare. Some experts indeed believe that it could well be considered our rarest butterfly after the Large Blue. Dr Morris and Dr Jeremy Thomas certainly do. It is a woodland butterfly which usually sticks to the woods and hibernates very soon after it emerges from the chrysalis, so it is very seldom seen – it is, though, a messy feeder, and leaves tell-tale marks of where it has been. (In 1904, Mr N. D. Riley found it commoner than the Small Tortoiseshell, at Wroxham.)

It hibernates as a butterfly in woodstacks or brushwood, awakening in March or early April. It performs complicated courtship flights for several weeks before mating. When ready to lay, the female flies high up into the branches of wych elm or the common elm, and after finding a twig she likes, lays her eggs on it, in a neat bracelet, gummed to the bark. The eggs are a light yellow at first, but they quickly darken to match the twig she has chosen. When they emerge, the caterpillars are gregarious, living in large companies, and they spin a silken carpet along the branch from which they are going to feed on the surrounding leaves. As well as elm trees they can be found on willow, sallow, aspen, poplar, whitebeam, and cherry and other fruit trees. They are safe from birds as they have sharp spines. When fully fed, they don't crawl down the tree trunk, but roll themselves into a ball and drop to the ground.

They pupate from the top of fences in fields, from ledges in farm buildings, and in tangled undergrowth and brushwood.

The female is slightly larger than the male, and with slightly larger markings. On the upper surfaces the wings give a tortoiseshell effect, being orange-brown with black markings, and are similar to the Small Tortoiseshell's, though not quite so bright. They fly powerfully, with intervals of gliding, and are sometimes to be seen basking in the sun, in lanes. They feed on pussy willow blossom in spring, and like the sap of trees.

The **Black Hairstreak** (*Strymonidia pruni*) is one of our most local butterflies, and, like the Large Tortoiseshell, considered by some experts to be definitely endangered, except on the few nature reserves that support it. There are probably only about thirty colonies in the country at present, and all are at risk unless specially catered for in the woods' management. Half the best colony and the whole of three more were destroyed in 1976–7.

This Hairstreak isn't black, but a rich chocolate brown! The females are larger than the males, and on the upper surfaces have orange markings all along the sides. Both males and females have a short twisted tail. They are difficult to find, for apart from being rare they are secretive and lethargic. They spend most of their time fluttering around blackthorn, but sometimes visit privet; they like honey dew, which is a secretion from aphids. In captivity they will feed on plum leaves. They rest frequently, with closed wings, and can be found in clearings in old oak woods, and along open rides, in Oxfordshire, parts of Buckinghamshire, Huntingdonshire and Northamptonshire.

The eggs are greyish in colour, and are laid singly on blackthorn; the winter is spent in this stage. The caterpillars hatch in March, but only when the buds begin to open into leaves. In two months they pupate, and the chrysalis looks exactly like a bird dropping. During their last moult they are said to feed all night and all day without rest or sleep. They can be seen in flight in June and July.

White-letter Hairstreaks, Large Tortoiseshell, Black and Brown
Hairstreaks on wych elm and blackthorn.
(For detailed identification see key on p. 62.)

This butterfly seems to be an exception to the rule that if its food
plant is common, it is likely to be fairly common too.

The **Brown Hairstreak** (*Thecla betulae*) is a very local insect
indeed. *Betula* means birch in Latin, but the name is not helpful as
the butterfly likes many kinds of treetop, as well as thistles and
bramble. It feeds largely on honey dew on trees. It can be found
locally round the Wash (where it is scarce), but it is more common, though still local, in Surrey, Sussex and Devon. It is a
butterfly of very secretive habits, and so is seldom seen, even in
places where it is most common. When it is sighted, however, it is
usually high up, in an oak tree. In sunshine it is lively, but in
cloud it becomes so lethargic it can be caught by hand. It can also
sometimes be found near bramble blossoms, and the female likes
to lay her eggs on sloe bushes or blackthorn. The males are a
darkish brown on the upper surfaces, with yellow splodges on the
forewings, and two orange tails extending from the hindwings.
The females have large orange markings on the forewings, and
like the males have two orange tails.

On the under sides they are light brown, and the hindwings
have two white lines, edged with black, running parallel across
them. The female is much brighter than the dull brown male on
the upper surfaces, though underneath the two sexes are very
similar.

The eggs are laid singly, in a fork at the base of a thorn, or close
to a bud of blackthorn, and remain as eggs through the winter.
The Brown Hairstreak is most easily found in the egg stage. The
caterpillars hatch in the spring. They are very oddly shaped,
being flat underneath and on the sides, rising to a ridge along the
back, so that from a head or tail view they seem almost triangular.
They are bright green, sometimes translucent, and have two rows
of yellow markings down the sides. They feed on blackthorn in

May and June and will eat the leaves of almost any kind of plum. Just before pupating they turn a purplish pink. The chrysalis is rounded, with a flat belly, and is ochre-coloured, marked with purple.

The **Lulworth Skipper** (*Thymelicus acteon*) is also very local. It is found only in Lulworth in Dorset (hence its name – which, however, was only given to it in 1890), the Dorset coast from Swanage to Portland, and in some very isolated parts of east Devon, but always near the sea. The sexes vary very slightly, the males having a thin curve of black on the upper surfaces of their forewings, and the females a curve of orange 'petals', or sometimes even a circle, looking almost like a daisy. Both sexes have their antennae tipped with black on the under sides. There has been at least one capture of a gynandromorph[1] in this species. They fly extremely rapidly, in a darting movement, and when they settle the forewings are raised and the hindwings are outspread, as with the Small Skipper.

The female lays her eggs in neat rows inside a thin sheath of slender brome grass. On hatching, the caterpillar surrounds itself with a thick white cocoon, and in this it hibernates until the spring. In the middle of April it eats its way out of the cocoon, and having demolished it, feeds on the

Lulworth Skippers on food plant (slender brome grass) in their habitat.
(For male/female identification see key on p. 62.)

young grass blades, making a shelter for itself by drawing two edges of a grass blade together with silken threads. It eats the blades round it, in 'wedge-shaped' pieces. The caterpillars are solitary, and like other members of the family eject their 'frass' or droppings a considerable distance from their lairs. They live as caterpillars for nearly eleven months.

The chrysalis, which is long and thin, is hard to see as it almost exactly matches its surroundings. It is fastened in its silken hideout by a silk belt fixed to the lining of its cocoon, and has a horn on its head. It remains as a chrysalis, according to Frohawk, from twelve to seventeen days, depending on temperature. The butterfly is on the wing from the end of June until early August.

The **Duke of Burgundy** (*Hamearis lucina*) – usually known as the Duke of Burgundy Fritillary

Duke of Burgundy Fritillaries, High Brown Fritillaries and Silver-studded Blues on food plants (gorse, violets and cowslips).
(For detailed identification see key on p. 62.)

-- is a dumpy little butterfly, somewhat similar to a Chequered Skipper in appearance, but it has a smaller body and no 'eyebrows'. F. E. Hulme comments rather crossly, 'It is unfortunate that this butterfly should be popularly classed as a Fritillary, and somewhat absurd that it should bear so sonorous and aristocratic an appellation. A happier name for it would be the Cowslip Butter-fly', and indeed the caterpillar feeds on cowslips and primroses. Hulme also describes the cater-pillar as being 'only twice as long as it is wide . . . like a wood louse . . . legs lost to sight beneath its corpulent sides.'

The eggs are laid in batches of about eight on the under sides of the food plant, and hatch in fourteen days. The caterpillars eat the upper part of the eggshell in order to emerge, and after coming out they finish the rest. They move very little, and feed by day, resting under the leaves. They pupate after only three moults in about forty-three days. The pupa lies along the leaf, tail downwards, and is attached to the food plant by a silken girdle and tail-hooks. It remains in this stage throughout the winter, and hatches about mid-May. Its lifespan as a butterfly is only fourteen days.

The butterflies are usually found in woods, liking best those in sheltered valleys or hollows, but they can also be found in places with scattered trees on grassland – and colonies do extend on to open downland. They are also to be seen in sunny rides or on pathways. They like the flowers of the wood-spurge and bugle; they fly low, and are very territorial about their favourite resting places. They are active, cheerful little butterflies, and it is sad that they are becoming scarce.

The **High Brown Fritillary** (*Argynnis adippe*) is a handsome large butterfly with orange and black markings on the upper surfaces; a typical 'Fritillary' in appearance. The females are larger than the males, and they are not so square-looking. Both sexes have a number of silver spots on the under side of the hindwings; those of the female being larger and more beautiful. They also have small silver spots on the under side of the forewings, but there are many variations, which can make things a little confusing.

They overwinter as eggs, which are laid in July and August on twigs, dead leaves or bracken, and there is one generation a year. They hatch in the spring, and the caterpillars feed on violet leaves by daylight, especially in sunshine. There are five moults, and the caterpillars move very rapidly. When about to pupate, they spin the leaves of the violets together to make a tent, and then hang on a silken pad by tail-hooks. The pupa lasts about twenty-five days.

The butterflies enjoy thistles and brambles. They are great sun worshippers, and at the sign of cloud fly into trees to perch. They also rest in the trees at night. The lifespan of the butterfly is about a month. They are only widespread in parts of Devon, where they may be locally abundant; in the Forest of Dean and the southern Lake District.

The **Marsh Fritillary** (*Euphydryas aurinia*) is a smallish brightly coloured butterfly, also un-mistakably a Fritillary. The sexes vary a good deal in size, though the female is usually larger, and her wings are more pointed. Unlike some other Fritillaries, there is no silver on the under side of the wings. There is a great deal of individual variation in this species; so much that it would be pointless to expand on the matter here, though in general one could say that the yellower butterflies come from the south-west, and the darker ones from Scotland.

The eggs are laid in huge piles of about five hundred, on the leaves of devil's-bit scabious, and hatch in about twenty days. The caterpillars live gregariously under a silken web, where they also eat. When the food plant is finished, they find another plant and live the same way. In August, after the third moult, they roll up some scabious leaves and spin them into a ball, leaving one or two holes for doorways. For some days afterwards they emerge in a party for a couple of hours in the middle of the day to feed, then return to their lair to rest. After another week they stay in the lair all the time, not emerging again until the early spring, when the scabious has grown fresh leaves. They moult five times, and have sometimes been reported as being so numerous that they 'darken the ground', but small wasps called 'hymenopterous' parasites are their bitterest enemies, and destroy them in great numbers.

When the time comes for pupation each caterpillar makes its own individual little tent by gathering leaves or grasses together, and fastening them into a point, with silk, and there the pupa hangs for fifteen days.

The butterflies, which fly for about a month in May and June, are rather lethargic, and love sunbathing with their forewings folded over the back ones. They are territorial, hardly ever leaving their own particular field, and liking yellow flowers of the Compositae family, like cat's ear, dandelion and hawksbit. If their field becomes overcrowded they can be seen flying singly along lanes or woodland tracks.

The **White-letter Hairstreak** (*Strymonidia w-album*) is one of my favourite butterflies. The sexes are very alike, though the males have scent scales, and shorter tails. Both sexes are brown in colour on the upper surfaces and a paler brown on the under surfaces, but here the markings explain the butterfly's name. A thin white line runs down the whole length of the butterfly and on the hindwings, and an almost perfect little W is formed in the middle of the line. (There can be variations, but this is generally so.)

The eggs are laid singly in the twig forks of elms (mostly of wych elm), and they overwinter like this until the following spring. After eating their way out of the shell, the caterpillars at once feed on the inside of the buds of the elm, which they enter head first, leaving the rest intact. Later they feed on elm blossom. (There is disagreement on this, some entomologists believing that they feed on the blossom immediately after hatching.) They moult three times, and during the last two instars feed mainly on leaves; they then pupate either on the sides of the leaves, at a fork, or among the winged seeds of the elm. The pupae, which last for about twenty-six days, are fastened to the food plant by tail-hooks and a silken girdle.

The butterflies spend most of their time high up among the elms, but unlike any other butterfly they have the quaint habit of crawling all over the barks of the trees, opening and shutting their wings as they go. They fluctuate greatly in numbers, some years having what can only be termed as a 'population explosion', and at

Marsh Fritillaries (top and centre: female; bottom: male) on food plant (devil's-bit scabious).

Large Heaths (top and centre: female; bottom: male) on food plant (white beak sedge).

others being decidedly scarce. They do descend sometimes from the trees, and then often in large numbers, to feed on nectar from privet or flowering limes. They like mustard, brambles and thistles. Their lifespan is about twenty days.

The **Silver-studded Blue** (*Plebejus argus*) was given its English name by Moses Harris. Before that it was called the 'Lead Argus', which doesn't seem to suit it at all. The row of silver dots on the under side of the hindwings is what inspired Harris.

The sexes are completely unalike; on the upper surfaces the males are blue with a black border and white frill on the outer margins, and sometimes black dots on the hindwings, while the females are a dull brown sometimes slightly powdered with blue near the body. The females also usually have a series of orange spots, forming a band on the outer margin of the hindwings, and sometimes on the forewings, too. The under sides of the males are bluish grey with black spots ringed with white, and the females are a brownish grey. Both sexes have a black-edged orange band – on the males, quite often only on the hindwings, on the females, on all the wings. The males are usually the larger, but there are many variations. The species hibernates as an egg, and there is one generation a year. The eggs are laid singly on gorse or broom, and take about eight months to hatch.

The larva eats its way out of the shell and feeds both by day and by night. It moves slowly in a curious undulating way, pushing its head forward and then drawing it back. It also eats heather, bird's foot trefoil, restharrow, and several other members of the pea family. When the gorse flowers die, it eats the new and soft young spines, and when feeding on trefoil it prefers to eat only one side of the leaf. It moults four times, and lives as a caterpillar for three months. The pupa, which lasts about eighteen days, is bound to the lower part of the supporting plant by a few random strands of silk.

The butterflies are locally common in the West Country on the coast, but most colonies are on the heaths of Surrey, Hampshire and Dorset. They live gregariously for about three weeks; they fly low, and are rather lethargic. They also spend the night gregariously!

The **Large Heath** (*Coenonympha tullia*) has three variants: Northern (Scotland), Central (Border and Northern England) and Southern (North Wales, Cheshire, etc). It is the latter, incidentally the most strongly marked variety, which is now at risk, though it is worth noting that the butterfly is not found south of a line from Cardiganshire to Lincolnshire. It is not at risk in Wales, only in England, the reason being the drainage of the peat bogs which are its habitat.

The male's upper surfaces are dark brown, with two eyes on each forewing and four on each hindwing. The female, paler in colour, has only three on the hindwing. The under surface markings of both sexes are similar: grey-tipped forewings shading into pink and then reddish-brown, with two eyes, and hindwings with a ring of no less than six eyes, giving the effect of an elaborate bustle. The sexes don't differ in size, but the males are nearly always darker.

The eggs are laid singly in July on white beak sedge, but in captivity they can be placed on fescue grass. They hatch in about fifteen days. The caterpillar, which emerges through eating a hole in the egg, feeds entirely at night, except on warm spring days, and has four moults.

The butterflies, which can fly very fast when frightened, are extremely active, and have a lovely dancing movement; they seldom seem to rest on flowers, though they can be seen on peat turves, and in dull weather can be found low down on grass stems or on heather. Their lifespan is between fifteen and twenty days. They fly in June and July.

They have several names. Lewin in 1795 called them the 'Manchester Ringlet' or the 'Manchester Argus', and Haworth in 1803 called them variously the 'Marsh Ringlet', the 'Small Ringlet', the 'Scarce Heath' and the 'Large Heath'.

And now we come to the last butterfly that I will write about here – the **Northern Brown Argus** (*Aricia artaxerxes*). It is very local in this country rather than rare. It is a charming little butterfly, classed as a 'Blue', though there is no blue anywhere to be seen. Both the males and the females are alike. The female has more bands of orange-red on all the upper surfaces, and has a larger band of orange on the under surfaces of the forewings; but there is considerable variation within the species.

There is only one generation a year, and they hibernate in larval form in the third instar. The eggs are laid singly on rockrose or storksbill, on the under side of the leaf, and near the rib. They hatch in about six days. The caterpillar eats a hole in the shell in order to emerge, then eats the remainder. It feeds both day and night until the third instar, when it feeds only at night, lying at the base of the food plant to rest, and going to the top of the plant to feed. It digs a small hollow in which to pupate, and spins a loose covering of silk for itself.

The butterflies fly in June and July, but only in sunshine, hiding immediately at the appearance of cloud.

It used to be thought of as a subspecies or variant of the Brown Argus, but between 1965 and 1968 Mr F. V. L. Jarvis of Bognor Regis and Mr Høegh Guildberg of Denmark showed conclusively

Comparison of the Brown Argus (top two, male) and the Northern Brown Argus (bottom two, male) on food plant (common storksbill).

that it is a separate species, and this was generally accepted in 1967. The butterfly is a deeper chocolate brown than the Brown Argus, and its localities are northwards from Derbyshire, Durham, the Lake District, Northumberland and Westmorland through to Scotland. It has become very rare, perhaps even extinct in its favourite habitats near Durham.

Notes

1. A gynandromorph is a very rare variation which is neither male nor female, but has some of the characteristics of both sexes; none of them is sexually functional, however, unlike the hermaphrodite which is always functionally male and female.

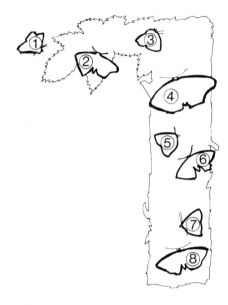

Key to illustration on p. 56
1, 4, 5 & 6: Lulworth Skipper (male); 2 & 3: Lulworth Skipper (female)

Key to illustration on p. 55
1, 2 & 3: White-letter Hairstreak (male); 4: Large Tortoiseshell (male); 5 & 6: Black Hairstreak (female); 7 & 8: Brown Hairstreak (female)

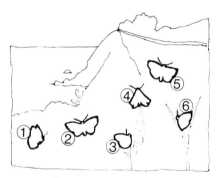

Key to illustration on p. 57
1 & 4: High Brown Fritillary (female); 2: Duke of Burgundy Fritillary (male); 3 & 5: Duke of Burgundy Fritillary (female); 6 & 8: Silver-studded Blue (male); 7: Silver-studded Blue (female)

RARE MIGRANTS

The word 'migrate' is derived from the Latin *migrare*, meaning 'to pass from one place to another'. It came into English use in 1611.[1] Before that, the word 'movement' was used, from the medieval Latin *movimentum*, but this was quite evidently less precise. 'Migrate' – and 'migration' too – should be used in a broad sense, scientifically.

Students of bird migration have for many years objected to the use of the word 'migration' to describe the movements of insects, on the grounds that a true migration must include a to and fro movement of the population between separate areas. In Chapter 9 of his book *Insect Migration* (1958), C. B. Williams, the great 'migration expert' who worked for many years at Rothamsted Experimental Station in Hertfordshire, explains what worries such students, and why. (See Appendix 7 for other quotes from this book and his *Migration of Butterflies*, 1930.)

The idea of 'migration' – in the term generally accepted by the public – has always fascinated me: why certain fish travel so many miles to spawn; why birds fly hundreds of miles to breed; why the Norwegian lemming behaves as it does, or indeed the snow-shoe rabbit; and why butterflies also travel hundreds of miles to come to these or any other shores. The Red Admiral comes here yearly in large numbers (in 1938 an assembly point for Red Admiral immigration was the sea-frontage of the Imperial Hotel at Exmouth!) and so does the Painted Lady; others very rarely. The more common species obviously find it worthwhile, but in the case of some of the others it is perhaps accident that brings them to us.

The **Mazarine Blue** (*Cyaniris semiargus*), for instance, was once indigenous here. In the first half of the nineteenth century it was fairly common, but it more or less died out in England in 1858; though in Wales, near Cardiff, it managed to survive until 1906. The last specimen recorded in England was in Sussex on 30 July 1958.

As a migrant it would be seen here in May to July, or again in August and September. It would be found on clovers and vetches, and also in gardens. On the upper surfaces the males are mauver than most other Blues, and the females are brown. The caterpillars have honey glands on their tenth segment, and like the Large Blue they are attended by ants – but this time the ants visit them. The butterflies always settle with their wings closed. As a species, the Mazarine Blue is still classified as 'British'.

The most spectacular of our immigrants is the **Monarch** or Milkweed butterfly (*Danaus plexippus*). Nearly three hundred are recorded as having been seen here. It is not yet certain how they come across the Atlantic, but it is known that they have been found in the holds of ships (so have their pupae). On the other hand, they do fly quite enormous distances overland in America, and most butterflies can rest on the sea if it is calm – so it is just possible that some of them fly here.

Some scientists believe it possible, especially those interested in *bird* migration, but Professor Urquhart maintains that they can neither fly in the dark, nor at very high altitudes, so he feels it would be an impossibility.

A. H. H. Harbottle disagrees vehemently. He estimates that if they did fly here, it would take them six days and six nights, using thermal (hot air) currents to get into the area where the

Long-tailed Blues, Mazarine Blue, Camberwell Beauty,
Monarch and Berger's Clouded Yellow.
(For detailed identification see key on p. 70.)

prevailing wind would help them. Mr Roy French, of Rothamsted Experimental Station, thinks they would take considerably less.[2]

Mr N. D. Riley thinks that there is no doubt that many are carried here by the winds from the Canaries, whence they also arrive frequently in Portugal. Roy French has enlisted the aid of meteorologists, who have plotted a wind track from Newfoundland to Cornwall, which he believes could 'pick up' Monarchs heading south on their autumn migration from the northern United States and Canada to Mexico, and divert them across the Atlantic. He accepts that only a tiny proportion of those that set out would survive such a crossing.

John Heath, in a letter, says: 'Almost all the records of the Monarch in Britain are in September or later, when this insect is migrating south from Canada and the northern United States to its overwintering sites in Florida and Central America. Therefore as this coincides with the hurricane season in the Caribbean some individuals are likely to be blown out to sea when they encounter the northern edge of the circulating winds, and will then be picked up by the westerly winds in the Atlantic and carried to Britain. Whilst not proven, this is the most plausible story. From reports over the years it seems that they sometimes rest on ships during passage. American birds also arrive in this country in the same way, and frequently at the same time.'

Whatever ultimately turns out to be the truth, one thing is certain: the Monarch is the only butterfly about which it is known that the same individuals make the autumn flight south in one year, and north again in the spring of the following year, in North America.

They have a wingspan of about four inches, and the upper surfaces are a brilliant reddish brown, with very pronounced black veining.

The Eastern and Central United States populations of the Monarch overwinter 9,000 feet up in the Sierra Madre in Mexico, within an area of twenty acres known locally as the 'Mountain of Butterflies'; there they stay until the time comes for their return northwards in the spring. They overwinter as butterflies in their millions, festooning tree branches, overlapping and covering the trunks of the oyal tree, and carpeting the ground in palpitating, fluttering, crowding hordes.[3]

The first specimen recorded here was caught in 1876, and since then the sightings have nearly all been on the Devon and Cornwall coasts.

Another beautiful migrant, from the Continent, is the **Queen of Spain Fritillary** (*Argynnis lathonia*). In Europe it is common, and there is a theory that the name comes from the days when Spain was a very rich country – the under surfaces of the butterfly's wings are studded with patches of gold and silver. It appears, usually in Kent, between May and late September, but there have been only two records in this century of its having bred here.

The **Camberwell Beauty** (*Nymphalis antiopa*), that butterfly of so many names, is now so called because the first capture here was in Coldharbour Lane, Camberwell. It either comes in ships, or it flies from Scandinavia. It seldom arrives until late summer, and has been sighted in most years, chiefly round Hull and Harwich, and other east coast ports. It has never been known to breed here although it has hibernated here, but those that do hibernate are thought to be so widely scattered that they fail to find a mate in the spring. It was first noticed here in 1748, and noted as relatively common in 1767, 1789, 1793, 1846, 1872 and 1880. Its greatest year was 1872, though in 1900 a further invasion took place; but until 1976 it was increasingly being considered as rare. In 1976, however, there was another invasion. It was seen first on 26 February at Snettisham in Norfolk (obviously this specimen had hibernated here) and the glorious summer which followed made possible the most extensive invasion in living memory. There were some 270 seen, but only about thirty-five were taken. In 1872, 150 specimens were taken. Perhaps the message of conservation is getting through to the public at large! In 1976 the butterfly also extended its range as never before, being found in Scotland, Wales, Ireland and the Isle of Man, as well as every county in England except Somerset and Herefordshire.[4]

The most likely places for it to be seen are in birch woods, or among conifers, though it will come into gardens that have buddleia and sedum. It is a large and lovely butterfly, its upper wing surfaces dark brown with blue splashes and broad creamy borders. The females are much larger than the males; both sexes have a glorious soaring flight, high over treetops. It usually feeds on rotting fruit and sap.

The **Long-tailed Blue** (*Lampides boeticus*) comes here from southern Europe. As its English name suggests, it has a definite and quite longish tail on its hindwings. It is a lively, lovely little butterfly, with a rapid flight, and it migrates singly. It is sometimes seen here in July, August and September, usually in gardens or public parks where lupins grow, on the south coast of England.

The one authenticated record of its breeding here was in a private garden in Torquay.

Its life-cycle is almost as strange as that of the Large Blue. The female lays her eggs singly, at the base of flowers of the lupin, the common vetch, the Spanish broom or the everlasting pea. When the tiny caterpillars emerge, they burrow into the blossoms, feeding on the petals, and after the first moult, they become cannibals, demolishing one another, until only the strongest are left. After the third moult, they burrow into the seedpod, feeding on the growing pods, but like the Large Blue, they have to be milked, and so they have a honey gland on the tenth

Queen of Spain Fritillaries and Short-tailed Blues on food plants
(wild pansy and bird's-foot trefoil).
(For detailed identification see key on p. 70.)

segment, which attracts the ants in swarms. Before pupating, the caterpillar turns from green to a drab pink, and after finding a dead leaf on its food plant, it spins a layer of silk, and a belt round its body, and becomes a chrysalis. Two weeks later it emerges as a butterfly.

The **Short-tailed Blue** (*Everes argiades*) is one of our rarest vagrants. On the upper surfaces the male is a violet blue, with rather darker veins, and its outer margins narrowly bordered in black and fringed in white. There is a short tail on the hindwings, which have some black dots on their outer margins. The female is brownish-coloured, becoming violet towards the base. There are black spots on the hindwings, some of which are edged on the inside with orange. The tails of the females are a little longer than those of the males.

It was first caught here in 1885 at Bloxworth Heath in Dorset, and is sometimes called the 'Bloxworth Blue'. There have only been fifteen recorded captures in this country, the last also being in Dorset, not far from Bloxworth.

It is a European butterfly, and it likes rough pastures, heaths and hillsides. Its food plant is clover, vetch, trefoils and other members of the pea family.

The **Bath White** (*Pontia daplidice*) is another rare immigrant from Europe. On the wing, it is sometimes confused with the female of the Orange Tip, because of the green marbling on its under surfaces. Seen near to, however, it is very different. It used to be called 'Vernon's Half-mourner', because the first British specimen was caught by a William Vernon in Cambridgeshire in May 1702, and this very specimen can still be seen in the Dale collection in Oxford. It was also sometimes called the 'Greenish Marbled Half-mourner' and the 'Green Chequered White', but according to Lewin who wrote about it in 1797 it was called the 'Bath White' (its present name) 'from a piece of needlework executed at Bath' by a young lady 'from a specimen of this insect, said to have been taken near that place'. Shades of Maria Merian!

Between 1850 and the turn of the century, only 123 specimens were caught here, nearly three dozen having been caught in the year 1872 alone. In 1945, however, there was an extraordinary influx. No fewer than 650 butterflies were either sighted or caught here in that year, mostly in Cornwall. A. H. H. Harbottle says that on 14 July 1945 several hundred of them landed at Looe where they fed, and then migrated on.[5]

The upper surfaces of the butterfly's wings are black and white, and strongly marked. If sighted here, they would more probably be butterflies from the second brood in July and August, than those in May, when the first brood are on the wing.

And now, almost last but not least, we come to the three Clouded Yellows that migrate to this country from Europe.

The males of the **Pale Clouded Yellow** (*Colias hyale*) are primrose yellow on the upper surfaces, and the females usually almost white, though yellow females have been seen. Both are tipped and bordered in a dark brownish grey, and have dark spots on the forewings; the male has a red spot on each hindwing. In both sexes the upper wings are black-bordered and the fringes are a pinkish colour. There have also been male and female albino specimens.

Like the Bath White, the insect is double-brooded, and in good weather conditions the butter-flies can be seen here in May or June. When this happens they lay their eggs here, and British-bred butterflies can be seen along with the new batch of migrants. The insect overwinters as a caterpillar, and, except in extremely mild winters, Britain is too cold for it. It is just possible though, that in very mild winters, a few specimens have bred here on the south and west coasts.

The butterfly flies fast, and its habitat is clover and lucerne fields.

Lewin was the first person to mention the Pale Clouded Yellow as a British species. He said he had found it in Kent in the middle 1790s. The best year for Pale Clouded Yellows was 1900, when over two thousand specimens were sighted.

Earwigs are very partial to its larvae.

Berger's Clouded Yellow (*Colias australis*) is so called because a Belgian entomologist, Monsieur L. A. Berger, was the first person to differentiate it from the Pale Clouded Yellow. He did so in 1947, and since then A. H. H. Harbottle and Mr A. J. Derwick have both bred it in this country. It hibernates in larval form, and Mr Harbottle has noticed that if the caterpillar is disturbed, it raises itself up and sways from side to side 'like a cobra'. In good years it breeds here naturally; it is a double-brooded butterfly.

In appearance it is very like the Pale Clouded Yellow, though it is paler and differs on the

Pale Clouded Yellows, Bath Whites and Clouded Yellows on food plants in a lucerne field.
(For detailed identification see key on p. 70.)

forewings in that the dark border is reduced, and on the hindwings this is often almost non-existent. The males are a slightly deeper yellow on the upper side, and a bright orange on the under side, but only experts could tell the difference between it and the Pale Clouded Yellow, except that its food plant is horseshoe vetch. On the Continent, to confuse things further, it often flies in company with the Pale Clouded Yellow. Mr Harbottle says it has a 'wilder flight' than the latter.

The **Clouded Yellow** (*Colias crocea*), like the Pale Clouded Yellow, favours lucerne and clover fields, but the two butterflies are easily told apart. Although it is subject to variations *Colias crocea* is an immediately identifiable species. The usual colouring is orange with black borders. Some of the males have hindwings shot with amethyst blue, and a white form (*helice*) of the female occurs commonly.

It is most likely to be found here in August or September, and was known to our earliest English butterfly writers as the 'Saffron' or the 'Spotted Saffron'. It is very erratic in its visits here, but its great year was 1947, when 3,600 were reported. Another good year was 1949, and so was 1955. The earliest time of year it has been recorded in this country is April, in 1956; and in a very good season a second brood of butterflies from these early visitors will be on the wing here in the autumn, and very exciting it is to see them! One was seen basking in the sun at Hove in *November* 1949! Alas, the cold of an English winter kills them off.

It can be seen, if it comes here at all, in most counties, and in Wales, Scotland and Ireland as well – even in the Orkneys. Its home is North Africa and Southern Europe, and in these climates it breeds all the year round.

A. H. H. Harbottle has a passion for the Clouded Yellows. He first became aware of one when he was about four, and attempted to catch it, but failed. When he was five, he disliked going to church very much, but his Nannie persuaded him that he must. On one particularly fraught day, when he had resisted and she had insisted, he returned home, and there in the garden was a Clouded Yellow! His Nannie ran out of the house and caught it, and he still remembers the delicious feeling of 'virtue rewarded' that it gave him.

He is now a royal chaplain in Windsor Great Park.

Albin's Hampstead Eye (*Junonia villida fabricus*) must be the rarest of them all; an Indo-Australasian butterfly, it has only once been reported here (and it is too rare to be included in the Check-list in Appendix 9) – I mention it here just for interest. James Petiver in *Papilionum Britanniae*, the first book ever to be devoted entirely to British butterflies (1767), says one was taken at Hampstead. In 1827 Laetitia Jermyn in the first edition of *The Butterfly Collector's Vade*

Albin's Hampstead Eye.

Mecum called it *Papilio hampstediensis*. In her second edition she classed it as a Satyrid (Hipparchia). It is now classed as a Vanessid.

Notes

1. See Professor F. A. Urquhart's paper, 'A Discussion of the use of the Word "Migration" as it Relates to a Proposed Classification for Animal Movements' (22 May 1958).
2. In a letter, Mr Roy French says: 'While I accept that Monarchs do not normally fly in the dark, I have no idea what evidence Urquhart has for saying that they cannot fly in the dark. Some of the records must result from continuous flight, day and night, unless you postulate that the butterfly lands and takes off from the sea each night and morning for several days.'

Mr French cites the following extracts from *Migration and Dispersal of Insects by Flight*, by C. G. Johnson, published by Methuen in 1969.

'But the marking experiments now leave no doubt that some individuals cover the whole distance and travel at least 2,000 miles (overland), and from records of Monarchs at sea (e.g. 700 miles from land, Walker, 1886), it would seem that a considerable part of the journey might be made in non-stop flight by some individuals.'

Johnson also says: 'Insects are usually seen to fly to within 20 feet of the ground, but they also frequently fly in swarms so big, that individuals are lost to sight.'

Mr French adds this fascinating piece of information: 'The Monarch has also crossed the Pacific, island hopping its way across to Australia and New Zealand.'

See the last part of Appendix 2 for Professor Urquhart's opinion.

3. Professor Urquhart wrote a justly famous article about this in the *National Geographic Magazine* in August 1976.
4. See J. M. Chalmers-Hunt's article in the *Entomologists' Record*, Vol. 89 (1977), pp. 89–105 and 298–9.
5. In fact, 1945 was a wonderful year altogether for butterflies; in that year, every butterfly mentioned in this book (apart from the Albin's Hampstead Eye) was sighted here. Among the immigrants, there were sighted thirty-one Queen of Spain Fritillaries, five Monarchs, one Short-tailed Blue and thirty-five Long-tailed Blues.

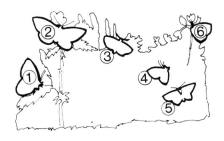

Top left: Key to illustration on p. 64
1 & 2: Long-tailed Blue (male); 3: Mazarine Blue (male); 4: Monarch (male); 5: Camberwell Beauty (male); 6: Berger's Clouded Yellow (male)
Top right: Key to illustration on p. 66
1 & 2: Queen of Spain Fritillary (female); 3 & 4: Short-tailed Blue (male); 5 & 6: Short-tailed Blue (female)
Key to illustration on p. 68
1 & 2: Pale Clouded Yellow (male); 3 & 4: Bath White (male); 5 & 6: Clouded Yellow (male)

8

A MISCELLANY

Why is a butterfly called a butterfly?

It may seem rather late in the book to raise such a question, but my husband, having read the preceding chapters, suddenly asked me, and although I have studied and loved butterflies all my life, I really had no idea. I in turn, therefore, asked many very eminent entomologists, none of whom knew for certain (nor to be truthful did they care!), so I set to work to try to discover why. What follows is the result, and it led me into many further researches, some of which are included here, as also are some facts which fascinate me, and which can't be fitted in comfortably elsewhere in the book.

★

'Butterfly is a day word, which suggests fluttering activity,' said Thomas Hardy.

★

> 'And what is a butterfly? At best
> He's but a caterpillar drest'

said Gay of *The Beggar's Opera* fame.

★

But why *is* a butterfly called a butterfly?

Dr Johnson believed it was so called because it appeared in the season of butter. There is also a theory that since the Brimstone butterfly appears very early in spring in this country, and the males are yellow, the Brimstone gave the butterfly its name. Alfred Werner in his *Butterflies and Moths*, 1956, would agree, and says specifically that the Anglo-Saxon word *was* their name for the Brimstone.

According to the *Oxford English Dictionary*, the reason is unknown! However, two possible derivations are offered: (1) From the Anglo-Saxon *buttorfleoge* (literally butterfly), so called after the yellow species, and (2) from the Old Dutch, *boterschijte* (literally butter-shit) from the colour of the excretion of the Cabbage White!

But is butterfly literally 'butter fly' in other languages? By no means, but the English name has links with the more complicated German story.

The German word for butterfly is *Schmetterling*. It derives from the Czech *Smetana* and comes to mean 'licker of cream' (literally 'what floats on top'), or 'butter'. There were many different dialect names including *Krautscheisser* (literally 'cabbage shitter') and *Milchendieb* (literally 'milk thief'), a name the butterfly shared with witches. In the eighteenth century under French influence it was for a while known as *Papillon*, but *Schmetterling* was restored to favour, and Goethe was a leading advocate of the change back.

The French word *papillon* is derived from the Latin *papilio*, itself according to Liddell and Scott's monumental dictionary a derivative of *palpito* (Latin) from the Greek *pallo* meaning 'to brandish'.

Thereafter things become more complicated. There is a theory that *pil* is a Sanskrit root suggesting 'hesitant movement', and Corneille in his great dictionary offers *papo*, to suck, as a rival explanation for the first syllable. *Papilles*, nipples or small sensitive scales on the surface of the skin, is surely another possible explanation. (Remember Dr Johnson's innumerable company of extreme small feathers.) Finally there was an early period when the *papillon* became a *pavillon*, literally 'a tent' (see the first paragraph of Appendix 7) or 'a small flag', another not inappropriate image – but like *Schmetterling*, *papillon* reasserted itself.

The Romans may have used *pallo* as a root for *papilio*. The ancient Greeks made no attempt to describe the insect's movement, colours or habits. As we have seen, they called it *psyche*, a word embracing the human soul both in life and after-life, thus linking up with much Eastern folklore and providing a bridge for it into parts of Europe. The modern Greeks, more pragmatically, call it a *petalouda*, literally a 'small leaf' or 'flower bud'.

In Russian it is *babochka*, a 'little soul', living in butterfly form after death. In Hungarian it is *pillango*, a 'creature of the moment'. In Spanish it is *mariposa*, a 'female-seeming creature' (*mari*) 'which alights' (*posar*). And, as a tail-piece which vividly illustrates the problems of entomological etymology, we have the Italian, *farfalla*. The dictionary consulted proposed the following ancestry: '*papilla* from the Greek *phalaina* meaning "a monster" or "a moth", which is clearly related to the French *balleine*, "a whale" '.

Whale or butterfly, creature of a moment or of eternity, little flower or butter-shit, witch or little flag . . . a wide range to embrace a small insect![1]

★

Butterflies are more truly 'sun flies', since they are so dependent on the sun. The sun is yellow, and butter is yellow, and to my way of thinking this is as good a reason as any to call them butterflies. The peak of their activity in a temperate climate is under the midday sun.

★

Butterflies are beautiful, and because they are so beautiful they often evoke feelings of awe. Helen Ignatieff, who runs the Canadiana Museum in Toronto, told me the following lovely story.

Her son was being christened in the Greek Orthodox Church in Toronto, on a wonderful sunny June day. He was lying back in his godmother's arms, crowing happily, when suddenly two large butterflies flew in through the open window. 'It was like magic,' she said. 'I felt the day had been blessed.'

★

Butterflies have affected many people very strongly, all down the ages. In Hindu mythology, it is said that Brahmah watched a voracious caterpillar in his garden turn into a pupa, and finally a butterfly, and his heart was filled with a great calm, and from then on he looked forward to his own perfection and reincarnation. Chuang Tzu, an eminent Taoist philosopher who lived in the fourth century BC, was known as the 'Butterfly Philosopher'.[2] In Malaysia, where I was born, and where Islam is the religion, there is a belief that migrating butterflies are making the pilgrimage to Mecca. (A butterfly there is called a *rama-rama*, or a *cupa-cupa* – both onomatopoeic names, though Rama in fact is an Indian god.) Virgin and Child paintings often show a butterfly in the hands of the Child: a symbol of resurrection. Belief in the butterfly as the soul of man is general in Europe, Japan, many of the Pacific islands and among many North American tribes. The Maoris believe that this butterfly soul returns to earth after death, and a tribe in Sumatra (which I visited in 1936 in an astonishing little river steamer whose Somerset Maugham-like captain never got out of his pyjamas, but pinned on his epaulettes with safety pins during the day) believes that the first three men ever to be born came from eggs laid by giant butterflies. Their wives were sent down later from above, to join them, fully grown!

The Serbians look on the butterfly as the soul of a witch, and believe that if they can find her body and turn it round while she is asleep, the soul won't be able to find her mouth to re-enter, and the witch will die. Funk and Wagnall's *Standard Dictionary of Folklore, Mythology and Legend*, where I found most of these myths, goes on to say that this concept of the soul probably explains why in medieval art many angels have butterfly wings rather than those of a bird. Luther said that the butterfly 'is an emblem of the devil in its crawling walk'. The Mexicans had butterfly insignia for both the Earth Mother and the Fire Gods, and in Hawaii there is a story very like the Greek myth of Orpheus and Eurydice: the story of Hiku and Kaweli. Hiku's beloved wife Kaweli died. Hiku went to the Underworld to fetch her, and found her spirit turned into a butterfly. He returned to her dead body, made a hole in her left foot, forced the spirit to enter, and she returned to life.

The ancient Greeks sometimes portrayed the soul as a diminutive person with butterfly wings, before they simply portrayed it as a butterfly. In south Germany some say the dead are reborn as children who fly about as butterflies (hence the belief that they bring children). The Slavs open a door wide to let the butterfly soul escape from a dead man. In the Solomon Islands the dying man has a choice as to what he will become when he dies, and he often chooses a butterfly. And among the Nagas of Assam the dead are believed to go through a series of transformations in the Underworld, and are finally reborn as butterflies. When the butterfly dies, that is the end of the soul for ever. In Burma, rice has a butterfly soul, and a trail of rice husks and unthreshed rice is put down between the field and the granary so that the soul can find the grain, because if it doesn't, none will grow the following year.

Among some peoples the butterfly is worshipped as a god, sometimes as the only god. A North American Pima Indian myth says that the Creator, Chiowotmahki, took the form of a butterfly and flew all over the world until he found a suitable place for man. Among some Mexican tribes a butterfly is the symbol of fertility.

Not all butterflies are looked on as good, though in Scotland it is unlucky to kill or keep one, and in the west of Scotland the white ones are fed. In Serbia and Westphalia they are regarded with horror, and in some parts of Germany they are thought to be fairies in disguise who steal butter and milk! So we come back full circle.

★

Mrs Quainton, who was the cook at my school in Wallingford and a passionate amateur naturalist, and who encouraged my early leanings, always called butterflies 'flutterbys'. 'It stands to reason they've got it the wrong way round', she would say in exasperation. She was the only

person to know how my snails kept on appearing on the cloak-room walls. She showed me where the 'school toad', as she called him, lived; and disposed of the tiny frogs that eventually emerged from the spawn I brought back in jam jars, having decanted the spawn into large goldfish bowls for me. She showed a keen interest in the diseased or deformed leaves I brought back from the school walks for her inspection, and acquainted me with the fact that snails are hermaphrodite – 'Ladies and gentlemen in the one', as she explained – and when I had measles at the age of eight, she lent me a copy of one of Fabre's books, which had, I remember, a – to me – ravishing picture of the dunghill beetle.

Once, to her passionate delight and mine, a caterpillar fell into my lap, when as a half-term treat I was taken in a rowing boat on the Thames. I managed to get it back to her in the pocket of my blazer. With its shiny green face, the toothbrush bristles up its back, and its jaunty red tufty tail, it was the joy of our lives, especially as she managed to keep it in a box with holes in it, until it became a moth. We thought then it was a Puss Moth, but Puss Moth caterpillars are entirely smooth, so it was probably a Vapourer Moth.

★

There is a strange and apparently ineradicable myth in this country that butterflies only live for a day. This is nonsense. No species lives for such a short time; in fact the shortest-lived survive at least ten days, even in unfavourable weather – for instance the Chequered Skipper, Essex Skipper, Grizzled Skipper, Mountain Ringlet, Small Blue and Small White. The Large Blue

Red Admirals, Green-veined Whites, White Admirals and Wall butterfly on food plants (hedge mustard, honeysuckle and nettle).
(For detailed identification see key on p. 78.)

and the Wood White, which also have unusually short lives in the imago form, are likely to live for about two weeks, the Orange Tip eighteen days, and several of the other Skippers, and the Small Copper, from eighteen to twenty days. The Small Tortoiseshell, which hibernates as a butterfly, sometimes lives for as long as eleven months to a year, while the Monarch has been known to survive a whole year in its natural habitats, and the Brimstone also lives as a butterfly for ten to eleven months. How the myth became prevalent, and why it still manages to keep such a hold on the collective imagination, I have no idea, but then myths are often believed more passionately than the truth.

The Ch'ing dynasty, which lasted from 1644 until 1911, considered the butterfly a symbol of longevity. The name had the same sound as the word meaning sixty years.

★

British butterflies are divided into eight families:

Danaidae	Only the Monarch (known here sometimes as the Milkweed)
Satyridae	The Browns
Nymphalidae	Fritillaries
	The Admirals
	The Tortoiseshells
	The Painted Lady
	The Peacock
	The Camberwell Beauty
	The Comma
	The Purple Emperor
Nemeobiidae	The Duke of Burgundy Fritillary
Lycaenidae	The Blues
	The Coppers
	The Hairstreaks
Papilionidae	Only the Swallowtail
Pieridae	The Whites
	The Orange Tip
	The Yellows
	The Brimstone
Hesperiidae	The Skippers

As can be seen, some of the families include butterflies of widely different appearance; they are accordingly divided into sub-families. (A check-list can be found in Appendix 9.)

As if this were not sufficiently muddling, some of the English names are highly confusing. For instance, among the Browns (Satyridae) is the Marbled White, because unlike the rest of the White brethren (the Pieridae) who use all their six legs, and have claws on their feet, the Marbled White makes do with only four feet without claws, and – another Brown characteristic – the female produces melon-shaped eggs.

The Duke of Burgundy Fritillary is out on a ducal limb by himself; a Nemeobiidid, not one

Top and centre:
Wood Whites (male);
bottom:
Small Blue (male) on tufted
vetch.

of the crowd of Nymphalidae. The rest of the Fritillaries have acorn-shaped eggs, with 'keel' bases; tubular-spined caterpillars, and angular chrysalides. The Duke has smooth spherical eggs, wood-louse shaped hairy caterpillars, and short, fat, rounded chrysalides.

Even the Red and White Admirals, though both Nymphalidae, belong to different tribes; the Red to the Vanessidi, and the White to the Limenitidi. In the eighteenth century, and a considerable portion of the nineteenth, they were usually known as the *Admirables* (yet in 1720 Eleazar Albin was already calling the Red Admiral, *Admiral*)[3].

★

'Butterflies are strictly oviparous,' said Brown, writing in 1833. 'There is an unerring foresight possessed by the female, that of depositing her eggs on the precise place where food suitable to the caterpillar after extrusion is found. With very few exceptions the eggs are enclosed in an adhesive cement, which fixes them to the spot on which they are deposited. When the eggs are extruded singly, this cement generally envelops each individual egg with a coating, as in the case of the Admiral Butterfly (*Vanessa atalanta*).

'There is a great diversity in the arrangement of the eggs after extrusion. Sometimes they are deposited in confused masses, but in general they are arranged in the most orderly and even systematic manner. The Common Cabbage Butterflies, with various other insects, place their eggs upon one end, ranked together in perfect order: by this arrangement, the larvae, which on hatching emanate from the upper end, cannot disturb the adjoining eggs.'

Albin, writing on the subject of laying eggs, said, 'To this end, they [the butterflies] do not lay their eggs loosely, so as to be driven from Place to Place (much less from Country to Country) by the Winds; but fix them on Plants which will be proper food for their *Worms* while in a growing state, and those that are laid only superficially on Plants are fastened by a Glew so tenacious, that the Rains can't wash them off. And as for those that are laid contiguous, they are not laid in a heap, but in exact Order, and so disposed, that one may not hinder the Worm of the others from coming forth.'

★

In the eighteenth century the Marsh Fritillary was known as the Dishclout or Greasy Fritillary, the wings having a shiny appearance that suggested the name; and James Francis Stephens, writing in 1828, says that in 1767 the Camberwell Beauty appeared in England in such huge numbers that it was called by the entomologists of the time the 'Grand Surprise'. In fact, Moses Harris had already called it by this name in 1766, though earlier entomologists had called it the 'Willow Beauty', and 'White Petticoat', and in North America, 'Mourning Cloak'.

'There have been several instances of the insects [the Camberwell Beauty] being found in different parts of the country in mid-season, as plentifully as the Peacock and Admirable butterfly. In 1793 in particular, they were seen in places as numerous as the common White Butterfly,' said F. E. Hulme in his *Butterflies and Moths of the Countryside*.

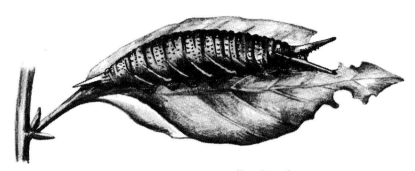

Purple Emperor caterpillar (x 1½).

Why is a caterpillar called a caterpillar? The *Oxford English Dictionary* gives the derivation as 'from the Old French *chatepelose*, "a hairy or downy cat" (cf. the Middle English *woubut*, "woolly bear", the name given to the caterpillar of the Tiger Moth), or perhaps because it was thought that *chatepelose* is the plural of *chatelpillar*, a "cat who pillages" '. I find this confusing myself. How about you?

James Duncan is slightly easier to understand. He says the derivation is French from the words *acat*, meaning food or provision, and *piller*, to rob or plunder. Just to confuse us a little, however, he says that the *acat* part, which was given to them on account of their voracious appetites, got corrupted into *cates*, and was used thus in Milton's *Paradise Lost*.

'. . . alas! How simple to these cates
Was the crude apple that divided Eve.'

Duncan goes on to add, 'Almost their only employment indeed is to eat, and so industrious are they at this agreeable occupation that they often in the course of twenty-four hours double their own weight in food!'

Catkins (French *chatons*) are another link between cats and caterpillars.

★

Oliver Wendell Holmes in *The Poet at the Breakfast Table* has this charming little exchange:
'I suppose you are an entomologist?'
'Not quite as ambitious as that, Sir. No man can truly be called an entomologist, Sir: the subject is too vast for any intelligence to grasp.'

★

Dr Miriam Rothschild claims that the female Large White butterfly has a way of assessing the amount of eggs it has laid. She wrote an extremely interesting article on this in *Nature* (Vol. 266, pp. 352–5, 24 March 1977).

The flight of Monarch butterflies has been timed, and it has been found that they can fly at twenty-five miles per hour, which is four times faster than the Large White. When the time comes for the migration of the Monarch, they all rise at a given and as yet unknown signal to start on their long, long flight. (Professor Urquhart thinks the signal might involve the angle of light from the ascending sun.)

★

The first person to give formal protection to a butterfly (the Apollo) was, strangely enough, the Kaiser, who was largely responsible for the First World War.

★

Toads and frogs enjoy eating certain caterpillars, and so do dragonflies.

★

The males of the Green-veined White smell of high-class verbena to attract the females, and those of the Common Blue, the Brown Argus and the Wall smell of chocolate.

★

Butterflies existed before man.

Notes

1. The word for butterfly in one of the minor Northern Nigerian languages is *Mallam-Bude-Talifa*, which means 'Wise man open the book'.

2. The following is an extract about Chuang Tzu's thoughts on death, from his *Three Ways of Thought of Ancient China*, translated from the Chinese by Arthur Waley:

'. . . How do I know that wanting to be alive is not a great mistake? How do I know that hating to die is not like thinking one has lost one's way, when all the time one is on the path that leads to home? . . . While a man is dreaming, he does not know that he is dreaming, nor can he interpret a dream until the dream is done . . . Once Chuang Chou dreamt that he was a butterfly, and was content to hover from flower to flower. Suddenly he woke, and found to his astonishment that he was Chou. But it was hard to be sure whether he was really Chou, and had only dreamt that he was a butterfly, or whether he was really a butterfly, and was only dreaming that he was Chou.'

3. The fact that Admirals and Admirables were interchangeable so fascinated me that I resorted to the latest Chambers Dictionary, and I found this:

'Admiral, *n.* the chief commander of a navy: a naval officer . . . Old French *a(d)miral* – Arabic *amir-al-bahr*, a lord of the sea, confused with Latin *admirabilis* (see next word).

Admire, *v.t.* to have a high opinion of: (archaic) to wonder at.'

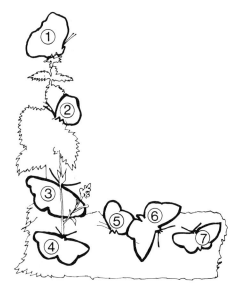

Key to illustration on p. 74

1 & 3: Red Admiral (male); 2 & 4: Green-veined White (female); 5 & 6: White Admiral (male); 7: Wall (female)

9

COMMON OR GARDEN BUTTERFLIES AND THE REST

So far I have only dealt with butterflies which are endangered or rare, for the obvious reason that it is these butterflies that most engage the minds of conservationists, but the butterflies most of us are likely to see are of course the common ones, and among them, thank goodness, are some of the loveliest.

There is no need to give more than a brief description of them, since all are illustrated in this book. (A page reference is given if the illustration does not fall within this chapter.)

By growing the right food plants in our gardens, we can be fairly sure, if we don't live in an urban area, that we shall see at least some of them.

Butterflies seem to be especially fond of mauve, and buddleia, in particular mauve buddleia, will attract so many, as indeed will mauve sedum (ice plant) – though not the variety called Autumn Joy – that by growing only these two plants, you are well on the way to having a butterfly garden of your own. Other favourites are wallflowers, polyanthus, lavender, honesty, Michaelmas daisy, golden rod, aubretia, valerian, phlox, scabious, alyssum, sweet William, sweet rocket, catmint, thrift, ox-eyed daisy, choysia and, if you are really keen, dandelions and blackberries. Single flowers nearly always have much more nectar than double ones. An orchard which in due course produces rotting plums will also help, and it is a good idea to have nettles growing in the vicinity, for the caterpillars of the Small Tortoiseshell, the Peacock and the Red Admiral.

Nettles always grow to cover the scars man has made. They cover the remains of a ruined building, or grow where rubbish has once been tipped, and the butterflies that choose to lay their eggs on them are also friendly to man. Small Tortoiseshells hibernate as butterflies, choosing outbuildings, sheds, and sometimes even attics to overwinter in. Peacocks become quite easily tame, and Red Admirals, which are migrants and find our winters too cold, sometimes nevertheless try to overwinter here in outhouses, but they nearly always die.

All these are spectacular butterflies. On the upper surfaces the **Red Admiral** (*Vanessa atalanta*) is a large, predominantly very dark browny-black butterfly, with white splashes at the top of its forewings, and diagonal red slashes across these wings. The hindwings have a band of red as a border. (It is illustrated on p. 74.) The **Peacock** (*Inachis io*) is a mauvy-brown butterfly, with a wonderful sheen, and four very large 'peacock's eyes', one on the upper surface of each wing. (It is illustrated on p. 24.) The **Small Tortoiseshell** (*Aglais urticae*) is a little smaller. It is a vivid

Speckled Wood, Large White, Small Tortoiseshell and
Holly Blues in the gardens of Buckingham Palace.
(For detailed identification see key on p. 90.)

orange-red, with yellow and black splodges on the forewings, and thin borders of black, blue
and creamy brown on the upper surfaces of all the wings. The upper surfaces give the impression
of tortoiseshell, which is how both it and the Large Tortoiseshell get their names, but it is brighter
than the Large Tortoiseshell. All of these butterflies have dark under surfaces on their hindwings,
and flash their bright upper surfaces wide open at the approach of danger.

Another visiting butterfly is the **Brimstone** (*Gonepteryx rhamni*), which arrives early in the
year. The males are bright yellow with a red spot on the upper surfaces of both the fore- and
hindwings. All the wings end in a little point. The females are greenish-white in colour, but
with the same red spots. (The chrysalis of the Brimstone, which is suspended by the tail, has
such muscular strength that if touched, it can throw itself upright immediately!) The difference
in the colouring of the males and females has led many people to tell me that they have seen
a Brimstone and a White mating. (Brimstones are illustrated on p. 21.)

The **Orange Tip** (*Anthocharis cardamines*), once known as the 'Lady of the Woods', is another early visitor. On the upper surfaces of each of its forewings the male has a brilliant splash of orange, the tips being dark grey, and the hindwings mottled in lighter grey. The under surfaces of the hindwings are marbled green and white. The female has no orange, and its markings on the upper surfaces are browny-grey and not so heavy. The butterflies fly in the spring. (Orange Tips are illustrated on p. 21.)

The **Painted Lady** (*Cynthia cardui*) is as ravishing as it sounds, and a doughty flier that covers great distances as a migrant. In 1879 a contemporary writer describes it as having come out of Africa 'in clouds that cast shadows on the ground' (for another account of migration, see Appendix 8). (Darwin, talking of migration, though not of the Painted Lady, describes in his *Voyage of H.M.S. Beagle* how he saw vast numbers of butterflies 'in bands, so that it was not possible to see the space above the snowing butterflies'. He said that the column flying 600 feet above the ocean was a mile wide, and he believed many miles long.) The Painted Lady is difficult to describe, for although she presents the appearance of being a kind of chequered salmon pink, many colours go to make up her glory. Once seen, however, she is unmistakable. White, pink and black are her main colours on the upper sides. (Painted Ladies are illustrated on p. 18.)

The **Green-veined White** (*Pieris napi*) is smaller than any of these, but not a little butterfly. Although at a superficial glance it looks like a Small White, its under surfaces are a yellowish green, the hindwings being very heavily veined in darker green. (It is illustrated on p. 74.)

The **Small Copper** (*Lycaena phlaeas*) is an attractive copper-coloured butterfly which has a brilliant iridescence to its wings. On its upper surfaces the forewings glow in copper, edged in brown, and spotted in dark brown, and its hindwings are dark brown edged in copper, with a row of black dots. Its caterpillar is stout, and lives on sorrel. It is very territorial, like the **Common Blue** (*Polyommatus icarus*), and the two of them have right royal battles.

The males of the Common Blue, which will also visit country gardens, are a fine lilac-blue on the upper surfaces. Like the Small Copper, their wingspan is between an inch and an inch and a half, and all the wings are margined with a thin black line and fringed in white. The under surfaces are buff and spotted, with silver blue at the base. On the females, the blue of the forewings on the upper surfaces is almost entirely obscured with a blackish-brown colour which turns into a band at the outer edge. (Common Blues are illustrated on p. 95.)

I found this enchanting passage in the Reverend F. O. Morris's book, *A History of British Butterflies*, published in 1893, the year of his death.

'We have few more zealous and pugnacious insects than this elegant little butterfly, noticed and admired by all. When fully animated it will not suffer any of its tribe to cross its path, or approach the flower on which it sits, with impunity. Even the large Admirable, *atalanta* [Red Admiral] at these times it will assail and drive away. Constant warfare is also kept up between it and the Small Copper Butterfly (which is also immensely territorial), and whenever these diminutive creatures come near each other, they dart into action, and continue buffeting one another about till one retires from the contest, when the victor returns in triumph to the station he had left. Should the enemy again advance the contest is renewed, but should a cloud obscure the sun, or a breeze chill the air, their ardour becomes abated, and contention ceases.'

In fact the Common Blue is so pugnacious that it is quite difficult to find an older one with its wings not torn or ragged!

The **Hedge Brown** (*Maniola tithonus*) or Gatekeeper as it is sometimes named, will call in if you live in the country. It is an overall bright brown with dark surrounds and 'eyes' on the forewings. In the wild it loves brambles. It is very common in the south, but only occasionally found on the east coast, and never north of the Humber. (It is illustrated on p. 27.)

The **Meadow Brown** (*Maniola jurtina*) will also call if you live in the country. The male Meadow Brown is a fairly large butterfly; the upper surfaces are dingy brown, with two tiny eyes on the forewings. The female, altogether brighter, has splodges of orange on the forewings and two much bigger eyes. On the under surfaces of the forewings both sexes have large, black, knowing-looking eyes, on a brightish brown background, and the hindwings are a drab brown shading into dark brown. (The Meadow Brown is illustrated on p. 24.) The **Comma** (*Polygonia c-album*) likes gardens, and is very easy to identify as it is a bright red-brown with black markings on the upper surfaces, ragged crenellated wings, and on the dark under surfaces there is a neat, very clear, white comma on the hindwings. They were once local, then became more widespread; there is currently a suggestion that they are decreasing, though 1976 was an exceptionally good year for them, and they even extended their range. The **Wall** (*Pararge megera*), an avid sunbather, likes gardens too. It is also a bright reddish brown on the upper surfaces, but the black markings are heavier. (It is illustrated on p. 74.) In the wild, in their remoter localities, the Walls seem to love companionship, and have a habit of joining in a walk by flying ahead, settling until one catches them up, and then going ahead again. When not sunning themselves on walls they can be found basking in warm corners of fields and shadeless roads.

The **Large White** (*Pieris brassicae*), once known as the Large White Cabbage, is a frequent visitor to gardens, and probably our best-known butterfly. It is about the size of a Peacock, but white. On the upper surfaces the males have dark grey-black tips to the forewings, and a few large black dots, and the females have blacker markings.

Hulme, whom I have mentioned already once or twice, absolutely hated the Large White caterpillars, saying: 'We have seen a garden with many hundreds of cabbages completely devoured by the caterpillars. They are of the number of those known in England by the trivial name of grub . . . From the astounding fecundity of these insects it may be wondered that they do not, in the course of time, completely overspread the face of the earth, and totally consume every green plant. This would certainly be the case if the Omnipotent had not put a check on their progress.' And he then goes on to describe their predation by ichneumon flies.

He also says: 'The caterpillars of the Cabbage Butterfly have a peculiar mode of climbing, which is either by a sort of ladder, or a single rope of their own construction, and so can climb up walls and glass windows. They leave a visible trail behind. The trail seen under a microscope consists of little silken threads which it has spun in a zigzag direction, like a rope ladder. The silk which comes from these spinners [spinnerets] is a gummy fluid, which hardens in the air.'

However, even the Large White is now having a hard time of it, and the Small White and

The difference in antennae (x 5) of Small Skipper (left) and Essex Skipper.

Butterflies that are doing well. Commas, Essex Skippers and Small Coppers on food plants (hops, sheep's sorrel and cat's-tail grass). (For detailed identification see key on p. 90.)

the Green-veined White have taken its place as our commonest butterflies. Dr J. S. E. Feltwell, the noted expert on the Large White, says that it is probably being decimated by a granulosis virus. The butterfly came to England from the Continent in enormous numbers in 1955, and Dr Feltwell thinks that the virus probably came with it.

The **Small White** (*Pieris rapae*) is like the Large White, but, of course, a good deal smaller. (It is illustrated on p. 27.) The **Holly Blue** (*Celastrina argiolus*) is the bluest little butterfly imaginable, having pale blue under sides spotted with black. The **Essex Skipper** (*Thymelicus lineola*), though scarce, is not confined to the county of its name. It closely resembles the Small Skipper; one way to tell them apart – if you are lucky – is to look at the under side of the antennae, which in the case of the Essex Skipper has some black. It is a small, bright brown butterfly with dark markings and a cream frill, and quite a large area of light but drab green on the hind under sides.

The **Speckled Wood** (*Pararge aegeria*) will only come to your garden if you have one with woods very near. It avoids strong sunlight, likes the damp, seems to do well in wet years, and flies from April until October. Although it seems to be decreasing it is worth an extra word here, because it is the only British butterfly to overwinter in two different ways, both as larva and pupa. There are usually two generations, but in hot years there are three, according to Sandars. Petiver in his *Papilionum Britanniae* called it the 'Enfield Eye' because he saw one in Enfield. Wilkes called it the 'Wood Argus', but Moses Harris renamed it the 'Speckled Wood', and the name has stuck.

The butterfly does indeed give a 'speckled' impression. The upper surfaces are a blackish brown in colour with yellowish spots, and one small black eye in each forewing, and usually three on the hindwings. The males are smaller than the females, and have scent scales, and more pointed forewings. The under sides are a pinkish brown, splodged in yellow, with an eye on each forewing.

Other butterflies will visit the garden but much more rarely, and naturally the gardens nearer urban areas attract less butterflies.

To get a comprehensive picture on the subject of butterfly gardens, read L. Hugh Newman's excellent little book, *Create a Butterfly Garden*. Mr Newman, whose father was also a butterfly farmer, and a noted dealer who sold many of his butterflies to Lord Rothschild, created a famous garden of his own at 'Betsoms' in Westerham. He was the man who advised Sir Winston Churchill on the butterflies in his garden at Chertwell. Mr Newman has also been responsible for interesting an enormous number of people in the subject of butterflies by the popularity of his books.

There is a public butterfly garden which should be mentioned here, because it is one of the loveliest in the world. It is called Drum Manor, and is in County Tyrone, Northern Ireland. It was especially designed to attract large numbers of butterflies indigenous to Northern Ireland, and to allow them to be observed easily in all their stages by the general public, as well as by naturalists, thus contributing in a very valuable way to the appreciation and hence the conservation of butterflies.

It shows how by combining formal and semi-wild gardens one can attract butterflies there in really large numbers. It is the first garden of its kind in the British Isles, and perhaps the first in Europe. It has three aims: to make an unusual attraction for visitors, to help conserve butterflies, and to educate the public in a spectacular way in the aims and ways of conservation in a familiar context – gardening.

It is not a zoo; the butterflies come and go at will, and they also breed there. A notable success has been the Wood White. For several years the staff had been preparing to introduce it artificially, then quite suddenly it established itself naturally. In fact the Wood White is a phenomenal success throughout Ireland. It has enormously expanded in range and in numbers, becoming one of the most common of the White butterflies, often commoner than the Green-veined White.

There are only twenty-six species of butterfly native to Northern Ireland, but some of them are slightly different in appearance from ours. The Common Blue is larger there, and more brilliantly coloured than anywhere else in the world. The Wood White, too, differs a great deal in appearance, and is an endemic subspecies.

Northern Ireland has a difficult climate for butterflies, even more difficult than England. There are less hours of sunshine, and the relatively high winter temperatures mean that the Peacocks and Small Tortoiseshells, which overwinter as butterflies, are not always torpid, which may cause them to use up their food reserves faster than they should. This, combined with the fact that there is not much wild nectar in the district in late summer (because of the dampness of the climate), means that it is harder for them to survive their hibernation. It is hoped that hibernation quarters which will suit these two butterflies can be introduced at Drum Manor, to help them through future winters.

One interesting fact has come to light. The garden was made from an old walled garden (the idea came from Mr F. Hamilton, who was then the local organizer for the Royal Society for the Protection of Birds), and it is obvious that such gardens are ideal for butterfly gardens. Because of the nectar shortage in Ireland, already mentioned, it has been found that garden flowers such as aster and buddleia supply the much-needed food for hibernation, and it appears that the growth of suburban living and suburban gardening since the middle of the last century has coincided with an extension of the northern limit of the Peacock butterfly!

Dr Henry George Heal, who is responsible for the above information, has been described as 'living for conservation', and indeed shares the responsibility for the considerable spread of knowledge, and therefore of interest, both in the Province and the rest of Ireland. His paper, 'A Summary of the Work at Drum Manor', was published in *The International Journal of Environmental Studies* (Vol. 4, pp. 223–9, 1973).

In February 1977, I had the great good fortune to obtain Her Majesty's gracious permission to visit Buckingham Palace Garden, the most famous in the world, in order to walk round it with her head gardener, Mr Nutbeam, to discuss butterflies. It was absolutely the wrong time of year to see any of course, but I could at least see the kind of habitat, and the kind of plants that were being grown there which might attract them.

I had to go in February, as my schedule for the year looked like keeping me out of London for a while; also, naturally I wanted to be as little nuisance as possible. In the event, the two of us walked around in the pouring rain wearing gum boots and with umbrellas up, while Queen Elizabeth the Queen Mother was holding an investiture in the Palace itself.

It is quite well known by this time that because of its size – 18 hectares (45 acres) – and its relative seclusion, the garden is a natural nature reserve. It is also equally well known that Prince Philip is a passionate conservationist. It may not be so well known yet that in April 1977 Prince Charles became the first Patron of the Society for the Promotion of Nature Conservation.

In the interests of entomology, Dr Bradley, of the Natural History Museum, has been given permission to make a collection of the moths and butterflies found there. He has caught the Brimstone, Large White, Small White, Green-veined White, Small Copper, Holly Blue, Red Admiral, Painted Lady, Small Tortoiseshell, Peacock, Comma, Speckled Wood and Wall. When you consider that Buckingham Palace is in the very centre of an enormous city, it is quite remarkable! In 1977 there was a startling capture of two Large Coppers. However, the prosaic explanation was that they had been released, together with four dozen others, less than an hour earlier, by a colleague who had bred them in captivity. Great water dock had previously been planted around the lake for their encouragement. To establish these gorgeous creatures in Buckingham Palace Garden would indeed be a triumph.

The garden contains among other plants about three dozen buddleia, and the same number of sedums. There is also a mercury-vapour light trap for catching moths (as there are so many more moths in Britain than butterflies) and the moth-catch has, I understand, been extensive.

It was a wonderfully happy morning. It transpired that Mr Nutbeam's mother and uncle had both been to the Hanwell Cuckoo School, in Hackney, with Charlie Chaplin, and that his wife's uncle had played with Charlie Chaplin in the school band.

Mr Nutbeam has now retired, after twenty-five years.

And so we are on the last run in, and to keep it all as simple as possible, I'm going to divide the other common butterflies that you may see into categories. These butterflies are unlikely to come into your gardens, but can be seen on your walks in the countryside.

A butterfly of the downs and limestone hills

The **Chalk Hill Blue** (*Lysandra coridon*) is a slightly larger 'Blue' than most of them, and is an iridescent ice-blue in colour, bordered with a white frill on the upper surfaces. (It is illustrated on p. 95.) It lives on horseshoe vetch in south or central England, or on the shore where such downs and hills fall as cliffs into the sea. It always has to be within easy reach of the ants that milk it.

Downland butterflies which tolerate but do not require chalk or limestone

The **Grayling** (*Hipparchia semele*), once called the 'Rock-eyed Underwing', is a large, dingy brown, late summer butterfly, with two eyes on each forewing and a much smaller one on the upper surfaces of the hindwings. It is local but fairly common and dislikes the damp. It rests on the ground with its wings always pointing to the sun, and is very difficult to see in this position. (It is illustrated on p. 24.)

The **Dark Green Fritillary** (*Argynnis aglaja*) is another local but fairly common butterfly. It is a medium-sized Fritillary, bright reddish-brown with typical heavy black Fritillary markings on the upper surfaces, and on the under surfaces it has a small amount of green on the forewings, with black markings and a row of small silver dots and a wonderful sage green with silver splodges on the hindwings. (It is illustrated on p. 105.)

It flies with great speed and power and is most likely to be seen on downland in the south.

The **Marbled White** (*Melanargia galathea*) is classed as a 'Brown', and has such pronounced black markings on the upper surfaces that it almost looks like a chessboard at a rapid glance. (It is illustrated on p. 95.) It hibernates as a caterpillar and pupates on the open ground. It can be seen in south and central England. It, too, is local, but fairly common.

The **Ringlet** (*Aphantopus hyperantus*) is about the same size as the Meadow Brown and is a dingy dark brown in colour with one black eye surrounded dimly with lighter brown on each forewing, and two black eyes similarly surrounded on the upper surfaces of the hindwings. It is common everywhere in meadows, hedgerows and woodland rides in southern England. (It is illustrated on p. 27.)

The **Brown Argus** (*Aricia agestis*) is in fact a Blue, though neither sex has a sign of blue on its upper surfaces. It likes chalky districts or sandy places inland as well as on the coast. The male is smaller than the female, and less colourful; the basic brown is duller, and the row of orange spots on both the fore- and hindwings is drabber in colour. On the under surfaces, the male is grey-blue, and its orange spots are pronounced and regular towards the edges of the fore- and hindwings. (It is illustrated on p. 61.) On the female, the orange spots on the upper surfaces have really become bright orange bands; the under surfaces are grey-beige, and again the row of spots has become an orange band.

The butterflies have a marked preference for the rockrose, but can also be found on hemlock storksbill. They love resting on the flower stems of long grasses, and strangely, since the Common Blue is a territorial little creature, they are often found sharing the same perches.

They are widely distributed throughout the southern half of England and in north Wales. They don't occur in Ireland. They are double-brooded butterflies; the first brood can be seen on the wing in May and June, and the second in July, August and early September.

The **Small Skipper** (*Thymelicus sylvestris*) is a lively little butterfly, measuring one inch across and, as already mentioned, almost identical in appearance to the Essex Skipper. The male is squarer-looking than the female, with paler margins edged in black with a white frill on the upper surfaces, which in both are a bright bronze. There is a narrow oblique bar near the centre of the forewings in the male, and his hindwings are darker than hers. Both are black-veined. The female 'wants' the black bar. (Small Skippers are illustrated on p. 99.) It can be found by sea walls and dykes in Kent, and is generally common south of the Mersey and Humber.

The male of the **Dingy Skipper** (*Erynnis tages*) is a little grey-brown butterfly, on the upper surfaces quite interestingly marked in varying shades of this grey-brown colour, but from the set of its wings unmistakably 'Skipper' in appearance. Its under surfaces are brown, dotted with white and bordered in darker brown, and the female is smaller than the male, and browner, with a greeny-brown colour on the forewings. (It is illustrated on p. 99.) It is widely distributed south of Yorkshire, where it is very local.

A butterfly of the hedgerows and wayside

The **Green Hairstreak** (*Callophrys rubi*) is so called because it is a really bright green on the under surfaces. It is the only British butterfly to have this brilliant green as a colouring. On its upper surfaces it is a fairly plain brown, and although it varies a good deal it is roughly the size of a Holly Blue. The male has a small oval spot of scent scales on the forewings, which show black when the butterflies are in their prime. (It is illustrated on p. 103.) The butterflies fly in swift, short swoops, and like to sit on the leaves of trees, bramble, furze or thorn. When they have chosen their territory, they always return to it. There is one generation a year, and they hibernate as caterpillars. They are the commonest of the Hairstreaks, and usually fly in May and June.

Butterflies of the woodlands

The **Purple Hairstreak** (*Quercusia quercus*) likes oak woods. The males are larger than the females, and are a dark purplish-blue on the upper surfaces. The purple is only observable in certain lights, otherwise they look almost brown. The purple on the female is much brighter, but is in a smaller area. Both sexes have little tails, and they are both a pale brown on the under surfaces, with a little white line, and a few black markings. They are enchantingly pretty. (The male is illustrated on p. 103.)

The **Silver-washed Fritillary** (*Argynnis paphia*) likes large woods but you can also see it on commons, and lanes where there are brambles and thistles. This is the largest of the Fritillaries, and has the typical Fritillary markings on the upper surfaces, though it is less square-looking than the High Brown. The female is the larger of the two, but the male is brighter, and has black scent scales along some of the veins. On the under surfaces there is as much green on the hind-wings as on the Dark Green Fritillary, but the silver marking is in broad bands, not in large dots, though there are two rows of black spots, some centred in silver, and also just inside the silver border of the wings there is a band of delicate pink. (The butterfly is illustrated on p. 105.)

The **Small Pearl-bordered Fritillary** (*Boloria selene*) likes woods that are damp, but also marshy ground and roadside hollows away from woods. It can be found on damp cliffs, too. Like the Silver-washed, its food plant as a caterpillar is the violet. It is roughly the size of a Hedge Brown, but again unmistakably a Fritillary, with its clear red-brown and black markings on the upper surfaces and the silver splodges on the under surfaces. (It is illustrated on p. 105.) There is only one generation a year except in hot summers, when there is occasionally a partial second brood; the butterflies are usually on the wing in June and July, though sometimes also in August and September.

The **Pearl-bordered Fritillary** (*Argynnis euphrosyne*) likes clearings in large woods, especially a few years after trees have been felled, where violets and primroses have begun to grow. It is only slightly larger than the Small Pearl-bordered, and is also a little less local, as its need for moisture is not so great. It rather confusingly likes to fly in company with the Small Pearl-bordered! The black markings on the upper surfaces are slightly less pronounced than those of its small brother, and there is less silver on the under surfaces of the hindwings. (The butterfly is illustrated on p. 105.) There is one generation a year except in hot summers, when there are a few butterflies from a second brood, so they can be seen from May until August.

The **Scotch Argus** (*Erebia aethiops*), which as its name suggests prefers Scotland, and only the north of England, can't truly be called a butterfly of the woodlands. It lives on rough hillsides, near sparse woods where the soil is damp, and the grass is long, but best of all it likes sheltered valleys which face the morning sun, yet are on the sides of woods. It is about the size of the Pearl-bordered Fritillary. The males, which are smaller than the females, are brown, with red bands on the upper surfaces of the fore- and hindwings, and in the bands are rows of small black spots, with white dots in them. The females are a paler brown; the dots on the forewings are much larger and have become 'eyes', and the bands are orange. On the hindwings, there is a repeat of the red of the males. On the under surfaces the males are again much darker, with little dots placed in pink bands on the forewings, and a white band on the hindwings. The females again have larger dots on the forewings, also placed in pink bands, and the bands on the under surfaces of their hindwings are yellow. (The butterfly is illustrated on p. 103.)

The butterflies only fly in July and August and only in the sunlight, retiring to the roots of the grasses at the first hint of cloud. It is said that the males of the Scotch Argus have 'a disappointed air' when they make advances to a dead leaf instead of the female because her camouflage is so good. They probably do!

The **Large Skipper** (*Ochlodes venata*) has a bent pointed tip to each of its antennae and is the only British butterfly to have this. It likes the rides in woods, wood sides, downs, rough ground, hillsides and cliffs by the sea. It is, as its name implies, the largest of the Skippers, and is not unlike the Silver-spotted Skipper in appearance on the upper surfaces, but on the under surfaces, since there are no white spots, the species look very different. (The Large Skipper is illustrated on p. 99.) Although it never seems to travel any great distances, it flies fast and with power, and according to Sandars, when it alights on the bushes, tall plants and grasses which it enjoys, it has the habit of turning round or walking for a little way with half-raised wings. In sunshine it rests with its forewings half open and the hindwings flat, but at night or when there is cloud, it closes its wings over its back. It is territorially aggressive to its own species.

The **Grizzled Skipper** (*Pyrgus malvae*), as its name implies, is a drab little creature, varying from dark grey and white, to black and white. The males and females are much alike, though the males have scent scales. (The females are illustrated on p. 99.) They aren't so dreary looking as the poor Dingy Skippers, for which I have a great affection because their sleeping position is so like a moth's, with bowed head, and wings in a 'cloak' position. Nor are they as drab as the Ringlets, which I also love, because they are so unafraid of man, and can be seen even in light rain; nor yet again as plain as the Meadow Browns (Ringlet-sized, but even able to fly in thunderstorms), but they can't be described as colourful. They fly however very fast, and jerkily, which is fun, and in sunshine can be seen happily basking. They rest on plantains, but don't seem to like other flowers. They are aggressive to others of their own species. Perhaps they can be described not only as Grizzled, but grumpy, Skippers.

These next three butterflies fall into more or less one group, and so can form a sort of coda to this chapter.

The **White Admiral** (*Ladoga camilla*) has probably the most graceful flight of all our British butterflies. It has been described as skimming 'aloft and alow' through woodland glades. It was reported as being seen in Essex as long ago as 1695, and still subsists there locally. Mr T. G.

Howarth has said in his *South's British Butterflies* that one was seen in Harlesden, London, in June 1952. It has vanished from some of its old haunts, but has spread to other localities, where it was not previously known. One of the extraordinary things about its flight is the fact that when flying among the trees, it sometimes follows the contours of every branch. It is a largish brown butterfly, almost black when fresh, roughly the size of a Painted Lady. The females are larger than the males and usually a little less dark (i.e. less blackish-brown) on the upper surfaces; otherwise the sexes are very alike. There are broad bands of white down the butterfly, making a V when its wings are outstretched. Both sexes are alike on the under surfaces, being prettily marked in brown and chestnut brown with a beautiful light blue near the body. There are the same broad bands of white on the under surfaces as on the upper. (It is illustrated on p. 74.)

The eggs are laid singly on honeysuckle, and hatch in about a week. The caterpillars feed during the day, and after their second moult, around the end of August, they make their winter quarters in a honeysuckle leaf by strengthening the junction of the leaf-stalk and stem with silk – eating off most of the leaf, and spinning together the edges of the rest at the base. They then lie along the midrib, with their heads towards the stalk, where they remain until March or early April, to waken and start feeding again. After the fourth moult they hang themselves up by their hindlegs and pupate in about thirty hours. The pupa, hanging by its tail-hooks on a silk belt, lasts in this state for around thirteen days.

The butterflies feed on bramble, and live for about thirty days. Both in wet weather and at night they rest under the leaves of trees.

Their chief predators are dragonflies and birds, though they seem to suffer less from parasitoids than most.

The **Wood White** (*Leptidea sinapis*) is another butterfly which is quite local, though encouragingly it seems to be spreading in some areas, and, as we have seen, it is having a great success in Northern Ireland. The Reverend F. O. Morris (1810–93) described it so beautifully in his *History of British Butterflies* that once again I can do no better than quote. 'It is,' he says, 'a very pretty object, floating lightly in the glades of the wood in a slow, undulating manner.'

It is a fragile-looking white butterfly, roughly the size of a Small White. The sexes differ in shape, the wings of the males being more pointed, with dark almost black splodges on the tips of the forewings, and the females having larger splodges but paler. (It is illustrated on p. 76.) The *sinapis* of the Latin name is misleading, as the food plant of the caterpillar is not mustard.

The eggs are laid on the under side of the leaves of tuberous vetchling, and on some other leguminous plants, and hatch in about eleven days; the larvae eat their way out of the shells, and then eat some of the rest. The pupa stands, tail-downwards, imitating the leaf of its food plant, which it resembles closely, and is attached by tail-hooks to a silken pad which it has spun on the stem. It is supported by a silk girdle. When the butterfly is double-brooded, which it is sometimes, the pupa lasts only eight days, otherwise it overwinters in this form.

The butterfly flies slowly and gently, in May, June and July, in wood clearings, settling on the flowers of the tuberous vetchling. It also likes heavily timbered forests as well as the paths and open rides where it flies from thicket to thicket. It likes shade, but will fly in the open, where trees have been felled.

If you are collecting one, and I hope since it is becoming scarce you intend no such thing – unless you are scientifically minded – *don't* put the little creature in a box or any form of container, as it will beat its wings to pieces.

The **Small Blue** (*Cupido minimus*) has also in its time been called the 'Sooty Blue', the 'Bedford Blue', and the 'Little Blue'.

The eggs are laid on vetch flowers, but only one to each head. They hatch in five to seven days. Sometimes a second female lays her egg in the same flower head and if this happens the stronger caterpillar eats the other when it emerges. They develop honey glands on the tenth segment, and after the third moult they spin together a few dead flowers. Then they hibernate and pupate, head upwards, attached by tail-hooks to a silk belt, which is a perfect camouflage.

The butterflies are a sooty blue-brown on the upper surfaces, and blue-grey underneath. Both sexes are about the same size (very small), but they sometimes have a dusting of quite definite blue on the upper surfaces, and the females are sometimes slightly yellower on the under surfaces. (A male is illustrated on p. 76.)

Usually there is only one generation. They are commonly seen in May or June, but in very hot summers also in August and September, from a second brood. They like warm hollows, chalk pits and quarries. They are very local indeed, fly fast, rest with wide-open wings, and if disturbed fly round and round their territory, anxiously, instead of leaving it. At night or in cloud they rest under the leaves of their food plant. In sunshine they can be found on grass. They live in the imago form for fifteen days.

Found everywhere

The **Small Heath** (*Coenonympha pamphilus*) is a cheerful little light brown butterfly, roughly the size of the Duke of Burgundy Fritillary. It is plain and brown on the upper surfaces, with a blackish line and a white outer frill. The female is paler and larger than the male, and the blackish line near the white outer frill of all her wings and the black dots on her forewings are not so decorative. On the under surfaces the forewings are brown with a small knowing eye and the hindwings are brownish near the body in quite a large area, with a small half band of pink going into white, and a greyish top. The Small Heath is very common, and likes every type of countryside where there is grass, even up mountains as far as 2,000 feet and down to the sea coast. There are several variations in the colour – even partial albinos are reasonably often seen. It is a lazy little butterfly, flying slowly in short distances, but it will fly in both sun and cloud in May and June, August and September. (It is illustrated on p. 27.)

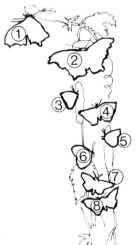

Key to illustration on p. 80
1: Large White (female); 2: Speckled Wood (female); 3: Small Tortoiseshell (male); 4 & 5: Holly Blue (male)

Key to illustration on p. 83
1 & 2: Comma (female); 3 & 7: Essex Skipper (female); 5: Essex Skipper (male); 4 & 6: Small Copper (female); 8: Small Copper (male)

90

10

PLACES AND PEOPLE

In *A Nest of Tigers* (1968) John Lehman quotes a letter from Edith Sitwell, in which she wrote, in the summer of 1944, 'I have just been violently slapped on the face by two butterflies. They were exceedingly drunk poor boys, and couldn't steer properly. Eventually they went back to their buddleia (if that's how it's spelt), the cause of their moral downfall . . . They were Peacocks . . . there were about fifty of them there, simply carousing, as if governments didn't exist!'

In fact, though the picture is charming, it is more likely that they had simply over-eaten. Red Admirals, Commas and Peacocks too can and do get drunk on fermenting apples, and they and other butterflies get drunk on other fermenting fruit as well; but the nectar from buddleia is their food.

Dame Edith wrote those words as an adult, but she was lucky in having had a garden throughout her childhood, in which, by the very nature of it, butterflies abounded.

Most people who love butterflies as adults were exposed to them in childhood. The eye of a child is delighted by natural beauty, if it has the chance to see it. To children, buttercups and daisies are more exciting than gladioli, a bunch of wild flowers picked on a walk more satisfying than asters, and dog roses more than garden roses; minnows and prawns more exciting than mackerel, and little inedible crabs as riveting as the edible ones. They love natural things, and small things. Butterflies have the added advantage that being 'sun flies' they are part of the idyll of a sunny summer day, and the first imprint of a butterfly on a summer day on the mind of a child is often what has stirred its interest in butterflies for the rest of a lifetime.

The late Sir Terence Rattigan, when he heard that I was going to write a book on butterflies, remembered suddenly with affection and enthusiasm the day he and his father caught a Camberwell Beauty when they were on holiday in Germany. Mr N. D. Riley lived next door to the great Richard South; as a child he became interested in lepidoptera when he saw a Tiger Moth for the first time. Nabokov, the Russian author, best known perhaps for *Lolita*, was also a collector as a child (as well as an adult). On being interviewed on his loathings and pleasures, he said, 'My loathings are simple: stupidity, oppression, crime, cruelty, and soft music. My pleasures are the most intense known to man: writing and butterfly hunting.'

As I've said before, amateurs in the entomological field have done as important work as professionals. Maria Merian convinced her contemporaries of the facts of metamorphosis, while Swammerdam was proving it scientifically. Captain Purefoy's experiment with the Large Blue was as important to entomologists as Frohawk's professional dedication and writing. Dr L. G. Higgins, who collaborated with N. D. Riley on *A Field Guide to the Butterflies of Britain and Europe* (which has sold more than 100,000 copies and has been translated into eight languages) was a successful gynaecologist, while Riley is a professional entomologist. The Reverend F. O. Morris wrote as good a book on butterflies as many of his scientific contemporaries, and though Monsieur Berger discovered that Berger's Clouded Yellow (*Colias australis*) was a different species from the Pale Clouded Yellow (*Colias hyale*), it was, among others, the amateur breeder the Reverend A. H. H. Harbottle who substantiated the fact, by noting the differences when breeding it in captivity.

Clergymen in fact have had a very good record as natural historians, perhaps because they are more ready than most to wonder at the marvels of the Creator (though Swammerdam would have been, and in fact was, the first anatomist to agree with them).

In *The History of Animals, Serpents, etc* by Topsel and Muffet, there is this marvellous paragraph (I've kept the original inconsistent spelling, except where 's' is printed as 'f' as this seemed too confusing – confufing!): 'He that beholds the forms, clothing, elegancy and rich habits, of the Butterflies, how can he choose but admire the bountiful God, who is the Author and giver of so rich a treasure? Wherefore art thou proud in decking thyself, and take so much delight in thy own beauty? Possess thy temporary fading goods without envie, for knowing that there is no butterfly but is as beautiful and plealing [pleasing?] and for the length of their life they have a more constant comeliness than thou hast: thou hast it may be an incredible agility of body, and nimbleness in running, but yet O man, if thou shoudest exceed all men, thou canst not equall a Butterfly. But you will reply that your cloathing is incomparable, and that you can boast of the *Persian* and *Tyrian* silk, of the best purple dyes, brought unto you by shipping: truly should you but see the rich robes of any Butterfly, besides their purple dyes and the rows of pearls, and the borders set with diamonds, rubies, the pyropus, opals, emrods; if you did but see and consider seriously the elaborate composition of their futures [features] and joynts and the imbroidered work here and there, of fine divers coloured twine silk, set with studs and eyes of gold and silver, thou wouldst let fall thy painted tail like the Peacock, and casting thy eyes down to the ground from whence thou wert made, thou wouldst learn to be more wise. It may be that thou wert born at first in a house of clay and mud walls, or else in a palace built of polished stones; but some butterflies are born in their houses that are the *Aurelia* like to pure gold, and exceed *Attalus* for the excellency of their birth, and delicacy of their apparel. Learn therefore O mortal Man, whoever thou art, that God that is best and greatest of all, made the butterfly to pull down thy pride, and by the shortness of their life (which is of no great continuance) be thou mindful of thy own failing condition.'

If, having had your interest seriously aroused about butterflies, you should want to know more about them, then it seems to me that there are several things to be done. Since they, like everything else, are far more interesting when you know a little about them, then besides looking out for them in your garden and in the countryside (and if you are in the fortunate position to do so, growing the right plants for them) I suggest that whatever your age group, a visit to the **Natural History Museum** in London is a good idea.

The Natural History Museum, formerly a part of the British Museum, is known as the British Museum (Natural History). It is housed in an enormous, Italianate building of light terracotta (made by Doulton) in the Cromwell Road. It is an utterly fascinating place, and is visited by vast numbers of people yearly.

The Insect Gallery includes a small, general display on the diversity and biology of butterflies and moths, and a detailed 'reference collection' display of all species of British butterflies, showing both males and females, and the upper and under sides of all of them. There is also a similar display of most of the larger British moths.

The frieze round the Gallery, of insects drawn in white silhouette against a dark glass background, is lit from behind, and was executed by Brian Hargreaves, as were some of the show cases round the room.

The very large research collections in the Museum are held within the Department of Entomology under the direction of the Keeper, Dr Paul Freeman, DSc. They aren't open for public viewing as they are primarily a basis for international research on the classification and biology of these insects, and together with the Library, form a major centre of scientific reference. The head of the Entomology Library is Miss Pamela Gilbert, a charming and immensely knowledgeable young woman.

Curation of the collections, and a great part of the research done on them, is carried out by the scientific staff of the Department. If you want to make any enquiries about the collections or their use, address them to Dr Paul Freeman, Keeper of Entomology, at the Museum.

Mr R. I. Vane-Wright, who is in charge of butterfly collection in the Museum, first became interested in butterflies on his seventh birthday. An aunt gave him a copy of one of Enid Blyton's books, and in it was a picture of some buddleia flowers covered in beautiful butterflies – Peacocks, Small Tortoiseshells, Brimstones, Red Admirals and so on. When a little later he went out into the garden, to his utter amazement he saw a buddleia bush covered in exactly the same butterflies! His new book had come to life! From then on he was hooked.

He says, 'It was my first real interest as a child, and I seem pretty well stuck with it now!' His chief research interest lies in the function of butterfly colour patterns and scents, and their role in the evolution of butterfly species.

Another fascinating place to visit, no matter what your age group, is **Worldwide Butterflies**, at Over Compton, in Dorset. It is the butterfly farm run by Robert and Rosemary Goodden.

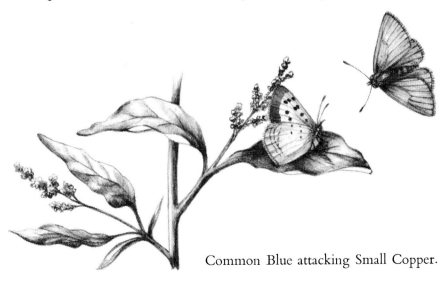

Common Blue attacking Small Copper.

Rosemary, if you remember, is the granddaughter of the great Captain Purefoy, so when Robert first met her at a party he excitedly told her that he too was by inclination an entomologist. She looked at him indifferently, and enquired, 'What is an entomologist?' Robert turned on his heel, and left her. Ten years later he asked her to marry him, and they now have the most successful butterfly farm in this country, and three children.

The farm is open to the public every day of the week; also at weekends, and on bank holidays. The last time I visited Over Compton, one hundred children with their attendant school teachers were there, too. It is usually very lively!

Butterfly farms are not found in every country, and in fact there is nowhere else in the world where you can find a farm of this size and scope, which supplies live butterflies, entomological equipment, and collections of dead specimens to almost every other country. It is a unique place for stimulating interest in living butterflies, and as such, should be taken very seriously.

The majority of people who buy butterflies are amateur enthusiasts who want to study butterflies in their own homes, and we all know how successful amateurs have been in this field. Schools use butterflies for education; so do universities, and specimens go to museums all over the world, while zoos buy eggs, chrysalides and insects for their insect houses. Butterflies are also supplied for release in ordinary people's gardens, and for restocking and conservation schemes, but in my opinion the most absorbing part of the farm is the fact that one can see butterflies of all sorts living, mating, laying eggs, the minute caterpillars breaking the eggs, growing larger and larger, pupating, and then emerging and drying their wings before flying off to re-create the cycle. Through the glass of the show cases, and also in natural tropical and temperate living displays, all this can be seen clearly and with far less effort than 'in the field'.

The place has, in spite of some initial difficulties, been so successful, indeed, that Robert Goodden has been able to take the brave step of buying back his own family home, Compton House (built about 1500) at Over Compton, to use as the farm in place of the nearby buildings that he had been forced to use before. The rooms at the north front of the house, which were a late Victorian addition (in Victorian 'Tudor') are the show rooms; the grounds are being replanted, and the massive walled garden and big greenhouses will be used for raising plants, and breeding species that have never been tried before at Worldwide.

Robert Goodden started out on his original plan to be a butterfly farmer in his spare time, when he was selling saucepans at Harrods.

Monks Wood National Nature Reserve at Abbots Ripton first became famous because an entomological dealer, called Mr Seaman, found some dark Hairstreak butterflies, and thought they were White-letter Hairstreaks. However, the great Edward Newman (no relation to L. Hugh Newman), one of the most respected of nineteenth-century entomologists, pronounced them to be Black Hairstreaks, a species new to Britain; so Seaman said he had found the butterflies in Yorkshire, to give himself a financial monopoly. This only worked for a short time, as in 1829 Professor Babington traced the real locality back to Monks Wood, where he caught a butterfly that year. Monks Wood then became the 'classic' site for Black Hairstreaks, and it became even more famous when four other Hairstreaks, the White-letter, the Brown, the Green and the Purple, were also found there.

It was declared a National Nature Reserve in 1953, and is made up of two woods, Monks Wood and West Wood. It is a typical example of ancient wood growing on lowland and clay soil, and is very rich in ash and oak trees. It covers 152 hectares (375 acres), and historical evidence shows that 111 of these hectares (274 acres) have been woodland thoughout recorded history. They are a relic of ancient woods that covered most of lowland England three to four thousand years ago.

Up to 1914 the woodland was managed as a coppice with standards (standing trees, usually tall, not supported by a wall), with an area of roughly eight hectares (nearly twenty acres) of hazel coppice being cut each year, on a twenty-year rotation. During and after the First World War the area was exploited by a team of Canadian lumbermen, who left devastation behind them.

Now as well as ash and oak there are birch, aspen, field maple, elm and hornbeam. There is also the rare wild service tree, and the shrubs include blackthorn, privet and hawthorn. There are flowers like the false oxslip (a hybrid between the primrose and cowslip) and a variety of orchids.

At the beginning of this century forty-three species of butterfly were known to be present, but in 1976 only twenty-nine species were seen. The White Admiral, however, is a local species, and the Wood White seems to be on the increase.

The Reserve is not open to the public except by permit; and thirty-four hectares (eighty-four

Marbled Whites, Chalk Hill Blues and Common Blues on food plants (black medick, cat's-tail grass and horseshoe vetch).
(For detailed identification see key on p. 100.)

acres) are being allowed to develop free from human interference where possible. Elsewhere there are paths for access on foot, and it is a very beautiful area.

Monks Wood Experimental Station is near by. It looks like a modern light industries factory, all glass and cream and brown paint. It is not a place for the general public to visit, but since it has some of the best entomologists in the world working there, it would be absurd not to mention it.

Dr J. P. Dempster is the Senior Officer. His principal work in butterflies has been on the population ecology and conservation of the Swallowtail. It was his grandfather who started his interest in butterflies, as he had a large collection. Dr Dempster's work is not strictly butterflies themselves, but what determines their numbers, and how far it is possible to control their abundance.

Our old friend Hulme said, 'In entomology, as in all else, as soon as one gets beyond the first smattering, one realizes the absolute necessity of staking out a little plot to work in, while sympathizing to the full with the workers in the other fields around us.' By and large, I should think that the personnel on the 'butterfly' side of Monks Wood would agree. As we shall see, most of them specialize.

Dr Eric Duffey is an invertebrate ecologist with the I.T.E. (the Institute of Terrestrial Ecology) and specializes in spiders, but in 1953 when he became East Anglian Regional Officer for the Nature Conservancy, his responsibilities included Woodwalton Fen, where he became interested in the Large Copper. He moved to Monks Wood in 1962, where he continued to study this butterfly, under caged conditions; his observations were published in the *Journal of Applied Ecology*. A further paper, published in 1977, described the re-establishment of the Large Copper at Woodwalton after the exceptional floods of 1968 caused its extinction.

John Heath is the invertebrate zoologist responsible for insect recording and mapping schemes in the Biological Records Centre at Monks Wood, and his maps showing the distribution of British butterflies are at the end of this book. Besides his book, *The Moths and Butterflies of Great Britain and Ireland*, already mentioned, he is the editor of the *Provisional Atlas of the Insects of the British Isles*, the Secretary-General of the International Commission for Invertebrate Survey (which is the co-ordinating body for invertebrate recording and mapping throughout the world) and a member of the I.U.C.N./W.W.F. (International Union for the Conservation of Nature/ World Wide Fellowship) Survival Service Commission, Lepidoptera Specialist Group. He is also the kindest and most helpful of men. ('Not always!' he commented on reading the book in manuscript, and deleted the sentence. For once I propose to have the last word.)

Dr Ernest Pollard graduated in Horticultural Science at Reading University in 1962, and followed this by taking a diploma in Nature Conservation at University College, London; he then obtained a PhD studying the insects of hedgerows. He is a joint author of *Hedges* in the New Naturalist series, and is working on the population ecology of rare invertebrates, as well as running the national scheme for monitoring population changes of butterflies. This is now in its second year. He has made a special study of the White Admiral in Monks Wood.

Miss Lynne Farrell graduated from the New University of Ulster in 1971, and has worked on ecological surveys in Ireland and Britain. She is at present a botanist in the Biological Records Centre studying rare species, but she has made a detailed study of the Chequered Skipper.

Wicken Fen, which includes **Adventurers Fen,** famous for its relationship to Swallowtails, is nearby, and is part of the Wicken Sedge Fen Nature Reserve.

Woodwalton Fen National Nature Reserve owes its entire existence to the far-sightedness of the Hon. N. C. (Charles) Rothschild. It is one of the only two fens in Huntingdonshire which are not farmed. Charles Rothschild initiated nature conservation in the United Kingdom by founding the Society for the Promotion of Nature Reserves in 1913. It was granted a Royal Charter in 1916, and in 1977 it was granted a new Charter as the Society for the Promotion of Nature Conservation. Reserves which present the insects' habitat were Charles Rothschild's idea. He acquired Woodwalton early in the century and from 1919 onwards the Society managed it and preserved much of its scientific interest in spite of rising costs during and after the Second World War. It also commissioned and encouraged the research and surveys which form the basis of management today. In 1954 it leased the Reserve to the Nature Conservancy, but is still represented on the advisory Committee. As I have already mentioned, it is the home of the Large Copper, which can be seen there on the wing in July.

Visitors have to have a permit to visit it,[1] and have to abide by the rules set out by the permit, because a great deal of long-term research is being carried on there, and experiments can be ruined by unwitting intrusion in the wrong places.

It is idyllically pretty on a sunny day, being utterly peaceful, with an area of 'droves', as they call the paths, intersected by dykes or 'drains', where the great water dock is specially grown.

The Institute of Terrestrial Ecology's Furzebrook Research Station is near Wareham in Dorset. It was the second research station of the Nature Conservancy, and for nearly twenty years operated under its aegis. In November 1973, however, the new Nature Conservancy Council separated from the Natural Environment Research Council (N.E.R.C.), and Furzebrook remains part of the N.E.R.C.

Furzebrook is in a sense a memorial to the first Director-general of the Nature Conservancy, Captain Cyril Diver. There is a story which says that one day Captain Diver and some of his colleagues were on their knees in the district, examining some obscure invertebrate on the ground, when they heard two passers-by talking. 'What on earth are they doing?' asked one. 'It's a new religion, and they are the first worshippers,' was the reply. In a way this was true!

The building is mid-Victorian, and surprisingly small for so important a place. It is 'famous' for its work on ants, and as we have seen for its work on the Large Blue. It believes its task is to do research which provides sound scientific information so that value and policy judgements on such diverse matters as coastal ecology, heathland, heathland botany and management, mites, spiders, bats and reptiles, and ants and butterflies, can be made.

Dr Michael Morris, the Senior Officer, is also the head of invertebrate ecology throughout I.T.E. He considers that he has been fortunate in coming into close contact with the work of Dr Dempster, Dr Pollard and Dr Duffey on butterfly population dynamics, as he regards this work as extremely important. He himself started a study of butterflies of the Porton Ranges in 1974. (Since 1969 the Lowland Grasslands section of the Institute has been involved with conservation studies on the experimental ranges of the Chemical Defence Establishment at Porton, in Wiltshire.) The Silver-spotted Skipper was found to occur there in 1976, but otherwise the area is most notable for its great abundance of common species.

Dr Morris went to school at Christ's Hospital, Horsham, where he became 'spontaneously' interested in butterflies. He says he was much influenced by Edmund Sandars's *A Butterfly Book for the Pocket* (so was I for the record), and also E. B. Ford's *Butterflies* (another of my own favourites). In 1954 he became a Fellow of the Royal Entomological Society, and in 1955 went up to Cambridge. In 1958 he won the first V. H. Blackman research scholarship to be awarded for economic entomology, at East Malling Research Station. After three years at East Malling he went to work in the Conservation Research Section at Monks Wood, under Dr Duffey, and in 1973 he obtained his present position at Furzebrook.

Dr Jeremy Thomas was born in Dorking in Surrey, one of a family of five children. He inherited his mother's interest in natural history, and had inspiring biology teachers throughout school and Cambridge, though in fact he says he was no more interested in butterflies as a boy than in other wildlife, and like most of his friends collected fossils and butterflies, watched birds, and kept a variety of pets, such as lizards, snakes, slow-worms, cats and dogs.

In the last term of his final year at Cambridge, he was so inspired by a series of lectures given by Dr Norman Moore on the application of research to wildlife conservation, that he asked if he could work for a PhD under him at Monks Wood. (At that time Monks Wood was in the forefront of wildlife conservation, and Dr Moore had the largest and widest ranging group of research scientists on the station.) Dr Moore agreed. Dr Thomas says that he was equally fortunate in being guided by Dr Dempster, who was then pioneering the application to conservation of research on the factors controlling insect populations, and he enjoyed his time at Monks Wood enormously. After gaining his PhD he was asked to join a new group specializing in population ecology of insects, working under Dr Dempster, and to specialize on the Large Blue. He did this first at Monks Wood, and then at Furzebrook, working in the field in collaboration with the Large Blue Committee.

Rothamsted Experimental Station in Harpenden is chiefly concerned with entomology only as it affects agriculture. It is in fact the oldest agricultural research station in the world and one of the best, with a staff of about eight hundred. The estate extends to 330 hectares (815 acres). Mr Roy French, a Principal Scientific Officer there, has the job of studying the movements of agricultural pests, but as his mentor was C. B. Williams, the well-known authority on insect migration, he too caught the 'bug'. As a boy, he was interested in natural history, but principally in wild flowers. He read botany and zoology at London University, and obtained a post at Rothamsted in 1948. He has been there ever since.

I think it is interesting to know what brought these men into entomology, and what they are doing for butterflies. I hope you do.

The Chequered Skipper Inn at Ashton Wold is the only pub in England which has been named after a butterfly, and probably the only one in Europe which puts aside a percentage of profit on every mug of beer or glass of wine sold, to further the increase of wild life!

Outside the pub, there is a splendid and accurate sign of the Chequered Skipper itself, made entirely out of nails by Brian Hargreaves's cousin, Paul Smith. On one side of the sign is the upper surface of the butterfly, on the other the under surface.

Inside, the walls of the bar are hung with posters of wildflowers, birds and butterflies from many countries, and above the fireplace there is an enormous model of a rabbit flea, because the Hon. N. C. Rothschild who built the pub was, like his daughter Dr Miriam Rothschild, an expert on fleas, as well as being, again like Dr Rothschild, extremely knowledgeable about butterflies.

In a wall cabinet upstairs there are the accoutrements of what is called the 'Old-fashioned Lepidopterist' – the clapper nets, killing bottles, pins and setting boards, and on another wall the tools of a 'Modern Collector' – field glasses, a camera with a zoom lens, cine camera and electronic flash.

With the descriptions 'old-fashioned lepidopterist' and 'modern collector' I entirely agree. Although many if not all of the entomologists at present practising began their scientific interest through collecting, there are now so many excellent collections on exhibition, and so many books with magnificent coloured illustrations which can stimulate the interest of any child who isn't going to become a scientist, that with butterflies on the decline it seems silly to encourage people without knowledge to pillage the countryside and make our environment even bleaker.

In Chapter 5 of his book *British Butterflies with Coloured Illustrations*, written in 1863, W. S. Coleman says, when talking about the catching and killing of butterflies: 'As for the first point, we have now the means of giving any insect an utterly painless quietus, be it capable of feeling fear or no.

'In regard to the second, I think few will deny that man enjoys a vested right to make use of any of the inferior animals, even to the taking of their life, if the so doing ministers to his own well-being or pleasure . . .'

How terrible – even if we give no pain! And the fright they receive on being caught must be considered pain.

Large Skippers, Dingy Skippers, Small Skippers
and Grizzled Skippers.
(For detailed identification see key on p. 100.)

Not nearly enough study has yet been made of the ecology of butterflies. Until the 1960s all the books were solely on the basic life history, and above all the collecting of lepidoptera. The conservation and the detailed study of the needs of butterflies are a new and exciting part of science. This is, it seems to me, a worthwhile direction for both amateur and professional lepidopterists. It is of course a personal view, and may be hotly contested.

To return to Ashton Wold. The story goes that at the turn of the century, a young butterfly hunter called Charles Rothschild was chasing Chequered Skippers at Ashton Wold, and fell head over heels in love with this particularly beautiful part of England. He decided to buy some land if possible, and contacted the local estate agent, who said that it was a quite impossible request as the owner was an eccentric, who never sold property, only bought it. When he asked who the landowner was, the estate agent reluctantly told him that it was Lord Rothschild – the young man's own father! (This was the first Lord Rothschild, not Lord Walter.) The story has a happy ending. The father let the son have what he wanted.

Notes

1. Permission is obtained from the Regional Officer for East Anglia, The Nature Conservancy Council, George House, George Street, Huntingdon, Cambridgeshire PE18 6BY. Visitors should notify Mr Gordon Mason (telephone Ramsey 2363) beforehand, as the entrance to the gate is usually locked.

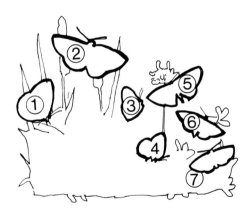

Key to illustration on p. 95
1 & 2: Marbled White (male); 3: Chalk Hill Blue (female); 5: Chalk Hill Blue (male); 4 & 7: Common Blue (female); 6: Common Blue (male)

Key to illustration on p. 99
1 & 4: Dingy Skipper (male); 2 & 3: Grizzled Skipper (female); 5 & 8: Large Skipper (female); 7: Large Skipper (male); 6 & 9: Small Skipper (male)

WHAT WE CAN ALL DO TO HELP

In our society most people work in towns, but an increasing proportion of them live in suburbs or in small satellite towns and have gardens of their own, so suburban gardens now constitute one of the major wild life habitats of the British Isles. Unlike most rural landowners, the occupiers of these gardens are under no economic pressure to use them in any particular way, so within limits they can grow what they like, and maintain them as they see fit. (So far, and thank goodness!) But how they use this freedom tends to be decided by current conventions – the example of neighbours, ideas picked up from television, gardening magazines, and the gardening columns of newspapers; not to mention advertisements. It would be wonderful if gardeners could be made conservation conscious, but the social pressures of 'neatness' in gardens means among other things that unless a professional gardener is employed, which is increasingly expensive, grass is giving way to crazy paving or patios, hedges to fences, and what grass there is, is sprayed with chemicals. It would be just as easy to change to more informal gardening, leaving wild areas, with wild flowers growing in them, and thereby encouraging wild life; lawns left just a little less cropped, so that thyme and dandelion could grow for butterflies (advice from both L. Hugh Newman and Dr H. G. Heal). Some of the garden, if it is a biggish one, could be made into an orchard, to provide rotting fruit (though a few stone slabs or crazy paving make good basking places).

Butterflies! Butterflies! Butterflies! They are the 'mobiles' of the garden, and so beautiful, and with such magical life-styles, that we would be the poorer without them. But how else can we help them, you and I? Britain in fact plays a leading part in Nature Conservation, but what about us, the interested public?

In my view, apart from gardens we must keep an eagle eye on what is being done to our surroundings. First we must know the kind of butterflies which inhabit the kind of countryside in which we live, and find out what is being done to that countryside, and the ecological needs of those butterflies; then, when we are on our rambles in likely butterfly places we know what we are looking for, and also what we are either happy or unhappy about. Next, we should join the local County Naturalists' Trust working for conservation, or the local Natural History Society, or support the very excellent Joint Committee for the Conservation of British Insects (which has also sponsored surveys of the Chequered Skipper and the Adonis Blue, among other butterflies). Under the chairmanship of N. D. Riley, the Committee has issued a pamphlet called *A Code for Insect Collecting*.

This is a very important document, and should be taken extremely seriously by anyone who has the interests of butterflies at heart. Here are eight of the stipulations:

'Consideration should be given to *photography as an alternative* to collecting, particularly in the case of butterflies.' (Here I would add drawing or painting as well, if one has any talent.)

'Specimens for exchange or disposal to other collectors should be taken sparingly or not at all.'

'Always seek permission from the landowner or occupier when collecting on private land.'

'Always comply with any conditions laid down by the granting of permission to collect.'

'When collecting on nature reserves, or sites of known interest to conservationists, supply a list of species collected to the appropriate authority.'

'Breeding from a fertilized female, or pairing in captivity, is preferable to taking a series of specimens in the field.'

'Never collect more larvae or other livestock than can be supported by the available supply of food plant.'

'Unwanted insects that have been reared should be released in the original locality, not just anywhere.'

Excellent, isn't it?

We can also join the society which has honoured me by making me a Vice President: the British Butterfly Conservation Society.

This was originally formed in 1968 by Mr Thomas Frankland and Mr Julian Gibbs. The idea was Mr Frankland's. Both are keen amateurs who felt that little had been done to co-ordinate or stimulate work for the conservation of British butterflies. They decided that they themselves should make a move, using their experience of other such society work. They personally provided the funds to start the B.B.C.S. and further support was given by the Frankland Trust. Thomas Frankland is a charities consultant, and was at one time a director of the Abbeyfield Society. Julian Gibbs, a merchant banker in London, had considerable experience of business and the financial side of trusts and societies; his father, when the Society was formed, being Chairman of the Nuffield Foundation. Julian Gibbs became the Hon. Treasurer to the B.B.C.S.

Sir Peter Scott was invited to become the President, and I a Vice President. Mr John Tatham is now the Chairman; and Robert Goodden, who was at first the Hon. Secretary, is now the Vice Chairman, and he and Rosemary are the joint Habitat Survey Officers.

Robert Goodden's connection with the Society leads some people to think that it is linked with his commercial butterfly farm, Worldwide Butterflies, at Over Compton. However, while his organization does everything to promote the Society, there is no direct connection between the two.

The membership is very widespread. The idea behind the Society is to preserve the habitats of butterflies, to make field observations, and to do breeding and research. In spite of the fact that butterfly populations depend on things beyond human control, such as climate and 'natural cycles', not to mention parasites and diseases, there is a need for such a society, whose work can help a little to prevent a further decline in our butterflies. For instance the Conservation Programme suggested for 1976 was extensive, and listed under three headings:

1. Habitat surveys.
2. Close study of endangered species.
3. Reserves.

Under the heading 'Habitat surveys', the Programme said, 'It must be emphasized that the basic knowledge of British butterflies has, up till now, been formed by amateurs and professionals whose observations have been made in the course of collecting and discovering life histories, and it is only in very recent times that serious thought has been given to the *conservation* and *ecological needs of the species for their very survival.*'

Just so, and the italics are mine.

Another paragraph runs: 'Weather is one of the most important factors . . . it would be important to record particularly good or adverse conditions during the flight season, flooding through the winter, or particularly extreme conditions at any time of the year. Early or late seasons should be mentioned. Changes of habitat by man are particularly damaging and detailed reports of any tree felling, planting, ploughing or other agricultural work, spraying, clearing, or undergrowth grazing, etc, will be of importance, and thereafter detailed observations of the effect, if any, on the butterflies, or relevant plants, or other ecological factors. *Watch* for the spread of any particular plant or choking undergrowth, attacks by predators or the presence of parasites which could affect the butterflies.'

Watch. That is a very good word.

The study of butterflies is by no means finite. Many, many things, some of them quite simple, have yet to be discovered. Why

Purple Hairstreaks, Scotch Arguses and Green Hairstreaks on purple moor grass, oak and gorse.
(For detailed identification see key on p. 107.)

do butterflies go for the colour mauve in a garden? Why do population 'explosions' occur? Is the scarcity that very often occurs the following year due to a resulting explosion of parasites? Has Dutch elm disease affected the population, already endangered, of the Large Tortoiseshell, or of the commoner White-letter Hairstreak? The subjects of migration and mimicry, not to mention defensive poison, are in their infancy.

A number of butterflies produce sounds, and certainly some can hear, too, but folklore has it that some butterflies are virtually deaf, while others are pretty sensitive to sound (for example, nymphalids fly off flowers at the click of a camera shutter more often than could be accounted for by coincidence). However, there is a problem here concerning *hearing* (differentiating pitches, etc) and a mere sensitivity to shock waves – effectively *touch*. Far too little is known about this as well.

Details of these things and many more are as likely to be discovered by amateurs as by professionals. Amateurs, as we have seen, have done great things. We must observe butterflies closely.

In that delightful book, *Bright Wings of Summer* (1976), David Measures describes how he watches for butterflies wherever he is, and how he draws them, and paints them, and photographs them, but never catches or kills them. His children photograph them too, and they do it very well. They stalk them with a camera, and can identify them, and are very knowledgeable about them.

Children make good photographers, and good watchers, too. They notice things more quickly than most adults and once their interest is aroused they are often more patient and more willing to spend long hours out of doors. A Mrs Coverdale from Ripon sent me two photographs her young son had taken, of a Peacock butterfly on some buddleia, which could hardly have been bettered by the best professional. Many children love drawing and painting, and are willing to spend any length of time on it when they become absorbed.

Children, too, are often the first to become keen on breeding butterflies, and since the butterfly population is declining, the ability to replace some of the damage can't be a bad thing. But breeding needs sustained patience, not patience extended over a few days, so if you are encouraging your children to get interested in this, be sure that they will not lose that interest half-way through.

Some butterflies are not difficult to rear, even with quite unsophisticated equipment. Plastic boxes make excellent rearing cages, for instance, though they should never be exposed to strong sunlight or the moisture from the food plant condenses and kills the caterpillars. The 'frass' (their droppings) must be cleared away often, otherwise it fouls the food plant, and the right food plant must be available in sufficient quantity, even if it means growing it in pots. It is also wise to know something of the habits of each caterpillar, otherwise tragedies can occur; for instance some caterpillars are cannibals (e.g. the Orange Tip) so they must be reared singly!

Most caterpillars will pupate on the top of the breeding cage, but some others need very precise requirements. Worldwide Butterflies will sell eggs, caterpillars or pupae. And information.

Probably the best way to rear butterflies is from the *caterpillar* stage onwards, as it is, I think, slightly easier than starting from the egg. If, however, you have decided on breeding from the egg, don't be surprised if it darkens just before hatching, and when the caterpillars do emerge, let them feed on their eggshells for a while, before transferring them to their (fresh) food plant. Either put a small quantity of the food plant into the cage, and move it when the caterpillars have crawled on to it, or pick them up very carefully on the tip of a soft paintbrush, and if you have a pot of the correct plant growing, put them straight on to this, and cover it with muslin

Small Pearl-bordered Fritillaries, Silver-washed Fritillaries, Dark Green Fritillaries and Pearl-bordered Fritillaries on their food plant (dog violet).
(For detailed identification see key on p. 107.)

tied underneath the pot to discourage parasites. If you prefer, however, you can put them into a larger plastic box (about the size of a sandwich box) lined with tissue paper, and put the fresh food on top of the paper. The box should be transparent, so that if anything is happening, you can see it easily. For instance, if you don't give the caterpillars enough food they will very quickly starve, and even if they are fed later, they are unlikely to recover sufficiently to get through to the imago stage. Incidentally, if you are using a paintbrush to move the caterpillars, move them one at a time, or you might injure them.

The food plant should be dry as well as fresh, and should be free of aphids' honeydew. Don't cram too much food into the box, and don't just put in an odd leaf or two and hope for the best, but arrange the food in an arc on top of the paper, so that the caterpillar can crawl all over it. Put a new liner into the box every day, as well as cleaning it out, but don't remove the caterpillars from the leaves or twigs on which they are resting; cut round them with scissors, removing as much old food as possible, and put the fresh food on *top* of the larvae, as they will always crawl up to it, but won't always crawl down if you put *them* on top. Airholes aren't necessary,

Chequered Skippers mating.

as there is enough air trapped inside the box, and the closed container keeps the food fresh.

Larvae that have been reared like this and are doing well can be transferred to a cylindrical breeding cage when they are bigger. This is ventilated through the lid, but these cages aren't made to stand in the sun either, or condensation may again result.

The best kind of cage is made with a wooden frame covered with fine netting, and can be home-made if the expense of buying one is too great. It is excellent for chrysalides – and the emerging adults too, because they can get a good foothold on the netting and climb up it to dry their wings – and this kind of cage can be placed near a window *without* fear of condensation. In a cage, potted food is less trouble than cut food, and better for the larvae, but if you have to have cut food, it must be stood in a jar of water put to one side of the cage. The food plant should be changed every three or four days, even if it looks all right, though if you are using pots, and stand a new pot beside the old one, most of the caterpillars will move over to it, and the following day the stragglers can be moved by hand.

In captivity parasites are seldom a problem.

There is a method of breeding called sleeving, but for sleeving, especially out of doors, and for hints on breeding from eggs (and if you do try this do remember that the caterpillars of the Blues and the Hairstreaks for instance are absolutely minute when they first emerge, so take care that you don't lose them by throwing them away), I would advise you to consult Robert Goodden's book *The Wonderful World of Butterflies and Moths* (1977) where you can get all the information you will need.

'What do you do about butterflies yourself?' I am often asked.

Frankly I take my own advice, though as a working actress, liable to move at a moment's notice from town to town, or even country to country, I seldom go in for butterfly breeding. My garden grows the right plants. I have my favourite walks where I know what plants will perhaps be supporting the eggs, caterpillars and butterflies that I may expect, with luck, to find in my particular part of England. And I read and read and read.

I know of few things more satisfactory than coming across an old book on butterflies and savouring its marvellous language – or a new one with the latest facts – except perhaps to be present in utter silence, in a remote peaceful place, on a sunny day, with butterflies surrounding me. In my garden the Peacock butterflies are tame. As an actress every night I have butterflies in my belly when I am working (I'm nervous at every performance, though I wouldn't change my career for the world) but as a person on most days of my life, at some period of the day, even in winter, I have butterflies on my mind.

And now to end this book, I shall quote my betters once again.

In his Introduction to *The Beauty of Butterflies* (1945) Julian Huxley wrote: 'If it be true that the highest and deepest in literature and art depend on a knowledge of human nature, it is also true that to avoid narrowness and false simplification, it is essential to have a knowledge and appreciation of the rest of nature that is not human. In particular, the realization of life's variety, or the existence of creatures that have their being in innumerable alien ways from ours, is a valuable corrective to self centredness, and an equally valuable promoter of that precious quality, disinterested wonder!' It's splendid, isn't it?

And this is from a letter from R. I. Vane-Wright of the British Museum.

'Man is interfering with the ecology of the Earth on a massive scale, mainly in blind ignorance or with total disregard for the consequences. Some people would like to stop this and return to the simple life. I simply do not think this will happen. Scientists should, I feel, devote themselves to studying the origins and dynamics of life, in all its manifestations, in the hope that this understanding will help us to co-exist with nature in an intelligent way. For this reason alone, quite apart from aesthetics, all species of animals and plants should be conserved. They are unique resources for understanding life, including our own life, and, ultimately for allowing us to continue our existence.'

So you see even butterflies play their part. They are beautiful. They sharpen our imagination, enrich our lives, teach us how to adapt to circumstances, and show us what enormous odds creatures can fight against, and yet survive.

Let us pray that the odds never become too great.

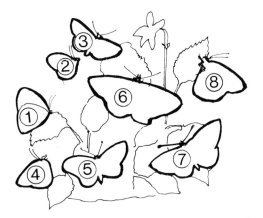

Key to illustration on p. 103
1 & 2: Purple Hairstreak (male); 3 & 4: Scotch Argus (male); 5 & 6: Green Hairstreak (male)
Key to illustration on p. 105
1 & 7: Dark Green Fritillary (male); 2 & 3: Small Pearl-bordered Fritillary (male); 4 & 5: Pearl-bordered Fritillary (male); 6 & 8: Silver-washed Fritillary (male)

APPENDICES

1. From Caterpillar to Pupa

After the caterpillar, or larva, has reached full growth, it finds a place to turn into a pupa, or chrysalis, its next stage of life. With the exception of the Skippers, which do not usually suspend their pupae but pupate within a cocoon, the caterpillar uses the liquid from its spinneret to spin a 'button' of silk on some solid object. This object may be a twig or the under side of a leaf. After the sticky liquid thread dries, the button stays firmly in place. The caterpillar grips the silk button with the hooks on its rear 'prolegs' (the abdominal legs, as distinguished from the thoracic, or true legs) and swings free, head downwards. Some caterpillars also spin a girdle round their bodies. The girdle serves as a safety belt, to hold the caterpillar close to the twig or leaf.

The pupa has already formed inside the caterpillar's skin. The pupa's thorax swells and curves, splitting the skin. Wave-like movements of the body roll the skin towards the rear, exposing the soft front parts of the pupa.

At the rear of the pupa's body, still covered by the skin, is the cremaster. For the sake of description, the cremaster may be divided into three parts: knob, shaft and base. The knob, which becomes attached to the silk button, is slightly larger in diameter than the shaft. Numerous spines, resembling button hooks, are its most characteristic feature. Being rounded at the apex, these spines are ideally suited for hooking on to the strands of silk contained in the button. The pupa has to slip the cremaster out of the old skin and hook it firmly on to the silk button, without falling. To do this, the pupa grasps the old skin between the folds in its body, then it pulls the cremaster out, swings it up to catch the silk button, and straightens out its body. The pupa is now completely free.

The outer surface of the pupa now begins to harden to form a protective shell. Some shells have strange shapes; many have bright colours arranged in patterns, and the shell often shines with gold or silver. Because of the golden colour, scientists use the word 'chrysalis' for this state. The word comes from the Greek *chrysos*, meaning gold.

The pupa does not eat, and is almost completely inactive, but inside the shell the greatest change in the whole process of metamorphosis of the insect takes place. The structures of the caterpillar change to those of the butterfly.

2. Professor Urquhart and the Monarch

Here is an extract from a letter written to me by Professor F. A. Urquhart, 30 August 1977.

'The evidence for the theory of Batesian Mimicry has been based entirely on caged birds and, for the most part, on two species only, namely the Florida Brush Jay and the North American Canada Jay. In my experience of fifty years of field observations I have never seen a bird attempt to eat a Monarch butterfly so as to find out if it is distasteful or not. I have seen male Monarch butterflies chase small birds, such as chipping sparrows, away from their particular guarded area but I have never seen a bird chase a butterfly nor has anyone ever published such records to my knowledge. I am strongly of the opinion that birds do not feed upon Monarch butterflies because of their remarkable similarity to birds in their flight, which does not activate a bird to eat it. Far more research is necessary, in the field, using many species of insectivorous birds, before one can accept the rather superficial research that has been done to the present time. The presence of cardiac glycosides, as proposed by some, is no indication of distastefulness to birds until proper controlled experiments have been carried out using many species, and, where possible, under field conditions.

'I am certain that some day the truth will out, and we shall find much that has been published is quite erroneous . . .

'From our research we have, I hope, definitely shown that Monarch butterflies do not fly to England. There is no question that they reach England on board ship, same as we do.'

3. Dr. T. A. Chapman and the Large Blue

The following is an extract from a letter written to me by Dr Jeremy Thomas, in August 1977.

'Dr T. A. Chapman deserves a mention in this connection, as he also discovered an association between the Large Blue and *Myrmica* ants, in the same year as Frohawk and Purefoy (1915). There had been speculation for many years about the possibility of such an association, but the species of ant was thought to be *Lasius flavus*, the yellow meadow ant that forms the ant hills, and most people thought the actual food of the larva was some vegetable matter; probably a root. In fact, Chapman found the connection slightly before Purefoy, when he accidentally killed a wild larva that he found in a *Myrmica scabrinodis* nest in May 1915. Its guts contained the remains of *Myrmica* grubs. That summer he introduced larvae to captive nests of *M. sabuleti* and *M. scabrinodis*, and observed milking and humping and carrying of larvae, but his stock died in hibernation, at the same time as Purefoy and Frohawk lost theirs. In 1915 he also definitely identified *Myrmica* grubs as the food of the young larvae, by analysing their frass.

'Old entomologists claimed that the Large Blue was particularly fond of laying on the mounds or ant hills of *Lasius flavus*, which may have given rise to the earlier belief that the ants were *flavus*. Two things were probably responsible for this misconception: *Myrmica* ants sometimes colonize old *flavus* mounds (but only a very small proportion of the nests in any given site), and thyme usually grows well on ant hills, and the Large Blues tend to choose the most conspicuous thyme flowers for oviposition [egg laying].

'*Myrmica* nests are inconspicuous, and are usually tunnelled straight into the ground, or under a stone, though sometimes there is a small pile of earth over the brood chamber, but this is never more than one inch high.'

4. Lord Rothschild

Lord (Walter) Rothschild (1868–1937), the 2nd Baron Rothschild of Tring, founded the Tring Natural History Museum, and was the last non-professional systematist to amass a large collection in more than one class of animal. His motives for doing so were the love of animals and the study of the problem of evolution.

A shy and delicate boy, he bought specimens of all the animals he wanted from dealers, and he was a very assiduous collector of insects. His father had an aviary, which probably stimulated his love for natural history.

At Cambridge, he met Professor Alfred Newton, who encouraged his interest, and from then until his death he was devoted to zoology.

After leaving Cambridge he went into the firm of N. M. Rothschild and Sons to study finance under his father, but he left in 1908, and then concentrated entirely on his passion for animals. At one time he had two and a half million set specimens of lepidoptera in his museum!

It was his acquaintance with Sir Walter Buller, who directed his attention to the New Zealand birds threatened with extinction, which stimulated his efforts towards conservation. Among his many schemes to preserve rare species was his purchase of the Aldabra Islands near the Seychelles.

The list of his scientific publications is very long, and much of it very important; from 1892 onwards there were no fewer than eight hundred papers or books, either written by himself alone or with collaborators, describing the flora and fauna of the world. His entomological collection is now in the British Museum of Natural History, in the Cromwell Road, London.

5. The Hon. N. C. (Charles) Rothschild

Charles Rothschild lived from 1877 to 1923. He acquired fame through his researches into Siphonaptera (an order of blood-sucking insects vitally important in the investigation of the transmission of tropical diseases – better known as fleas) and as the founder of the Society for the Promotion of Nature Reserves (now called the Society for the Promotion of Nature Conservation). He was the brother of Lord Walter Rothschild and the father of Dr Miriam Rothschild.

He was a sincere lover of nature in all its forms, and an enthusiastic collector. He realized the great importance of a thorough exploration of the flora and fauna of every country, and of securing the necessary steps in protecting not only rare or localized forms of life from extinction, but also in conserving their habitat and their essential setting, against the threat of changes in land management and cultivation, or of injudicious collecting. As well as the Society for the Promotion of Nature Conservation, the Commonwealth Institute of Entomology (previously known as the Imperial Bureau of Entomology) almost owes its existence to him.

6. Lady Glanville

Denzil Ffennell wrote to me two days before his death, with the following information about references to Lady Glanville given in a paper by R. S. Wilkinson in the *Entomologist's Record and Journal of Variation*, vol 87, p. 298, 1975.

Bristowe, W. S. 'The Life of a Distinguished Woman Naturalist, Eleanor Glanville (circa 1654–1709)'; *Entomologist's Gazette*, vol 18, pp. 202–211, 1966.
British Library: Sloane Ms 4066.
Harris, M. *The Aurelian* (London, 1776).
Petiver, J. *Musei Petiveriani centuria nona e decima* (London, 1703).
Wilkinson, R. S. 'Elizabeth Glanville, an Early English Entomologist'; *Entomologist's Gazette*, vol 17, pp. 149–60, 1965.

Note: Eleanor Glanville and Elizabeth Glanville were the same woman, but there is confusion over her name as well as her dates.

7. C. B. Williams on Migration

In his two splendid books, *Insect Migration* and *Migration of Butterflies*, C. B. Williams quotes two very interesting records of migration from the twelfth century. 'According to Schnürrer,' he says, 'in the year 1100, there was seen passing from the direction of Saxony to Bavaria, swarms of insects, which from their resemblance of their outspread wings to tents, were called "Papilloren".'

In 1104 there was another great flight, and Moufet had this to say about it (Moufet is the same man as Muffet, who wrote *The History of Animals, Serpents, etc* with Topsel, and indeed as Moffett, who wrote the treatise for Sir Theodore de Mayerne in 1634 – both Moffett and Muffet became corrupted to Moufet and Mouffet): 'Wert thou as strong as Milo and wert fenced and guarded about with a host of giants for force and for valour, remember such an army was put to worst by an army of butterflies, flying like troops in the air, in the year 1104, and they hid the light of the sun like a cloud . . .'

Williams has three more fascinating quotes. In Turpyn's 'Chronicles in the reigns of Henry VII and Henry VIII', he found the following paragraph: '. . . 1508, the 23rd year of Henry the 7, the 9 of July being relyke Sonday, there was sene at Calleys [Calais], an innumerable swarme of whit butterflies coming out of the north este and flying south-estewards, so thicke as flakes of snowe, that men being a shutynge in St Petar's fields without the towne of Calleys could not see the towne at foure of the clock in the afternone, they flew so highe and so thicke.' Williams goes on to say, 'There is no doubt that this refers to the Large Cabbage White Butterfly (*Pieris brassicae* L.) as the date (allowing for the alteration in the calendar) and the direction of flight, are quite in agreement with our modern observations on this species.'

In June 1464, Christopher Columbus, on his second voyage of exploration, wrote, 'Bearing up close to Cuba, they saw turtles of vast bigness . . . and the next day such immense swarms of butterflies as even to darken the sky.'

And one last quote from Williams, from his *Migration of Butterflies*, in the section on the 'Various Types of Migratory Flights': 'A thick cloud which in its extreme form, may "hold up motor cars", "cast a shadow on the ground", "cause turkeys to gobble in consternation", "or necessitate natives walking with their heads bent to the storm".'

In connection with migration, Charles Lane's article, already cited in my Acknowledgements and called 'Insect Migration on the North Coast of France' (*Entomologist's Monthly Magazine*, Vol. 91, January 1956), is well worth reading. Although he was only eight years old at the time, it is very entertaining. His observations were acute and true, and what he saw was carefully and lovingly recorded.

8. A Painted Lady Migration

In a minute to his colleagues at the Butterfly Migration Observation Centre at Zurich, on 31 January 1950, Dr R. Loelinger wrote as follows:

'We received on 19th September a letter from a new young member of our observer group, Otto Egli, of Basle, in which he gave us the news of an observation he made in North Africa in 1948. He writes: "As I worked in a travel bureau, I often had opportunities for going abroad. About a year ago I made the following interesting observation on the North African coast, near Tipiza (West of Algiers). In the morning I was lying on the beach of the Mediterranean. The steep banks were thickly covered with dry thistles. On each plant hung chrysalides of Painted Ladies, all formed up ready to emerge. After a short while, about half an hour or so, the butterflies emerged. After a further hour they were all fully expanded, and shortly afterwards as if on a word of command, the whole mass rose and flew in a cloud out over the Mediterranean."

'After some enquiries Herr Egli sent us this further information. "The date was 3rd of June, 1948. The weather was very fine. It was about 9 o'clock in the morning when I first saw butterflies emerge, so that by 10.30 practically all the butterflies were hanging from the thistles, ready to fly. Shortly afterwards the whole swarm rose, as I already said, like at a word of command, to fly out to sea. I calculated that the swarm contained about 2,000 insects. They flew as mentioned, in a cloud-like formation, about 100 metres wide. This comparatively narrow formation was of course only arrived at after they were over the sea. Previously the butterflies were spread out over a stretch of coast 2–3 kilometres long. They flew in a north-easterly direction and should, in all probability, have reached Sardinia by the evening. Whether *all* the butterflies flew away, or whether some of them turned back, I am afraid I cannot say after all this time." (Letter of 30th September 1949.)'

This was circulated by Captain T. Dannreuther, R.N., F.R.E.S., of Hastings, to members of the South Eastern Union of Scientific Societies, on 21 February 1950.

9. *The Classification of British Butterflies*
This classified list follows that in a Log-book Check-list of British Lepidoptera, by Mr Steve Fletcher and Dr J. D. Bradley.

Family: HESPERIIDAE (The Skippers)
Sub-family: HESPERIINAE

Chequered Skipper	*Carterocephalus palaemon* Pallas
Small Skipper	*Thymelicus sylvestris* Poda
Essex Skipper	*Thymelicus lineola* Ochsenheimer
Lulworth Skipper	*Thymelicus acteon* Rottemburg
Silver-spotted Skipper	*Hesperia comma* Linnaeus
Large Skipper	*Ochlodes venata* Bremer and Grey

Sub-family: PYRGINAE

Dingy Skipper	*Erynnis tages* Linnaeus
Grizzled Skipper	*Pyrgus malvae* Linnaeus

Family: PAPILIONIDAE

Swallowtail	*Papilio machaon* Linnaeus

Family: PIERIDAE (The Whites and Yellows)
Sub-family: DISMORPHIINAE

Wood White	*Leptidea sinapis* Linnaeus

Sub-family: COLIADINAE

Pale Clouded Yellow	*Colias hyale* Linnaeus
Berger's Clouded Yellow	*Colias australis* Verity
Clouded Yellow	*Colias crocea* Geoffroy
Brimstone	*Gonepteryx rhamni* Linnaeus

Sub-family: PIERINAE

Black-veined White	*Aporia crataegi* Linnaeus
Large White	*Pieris brassicae* Linnaeus
Small White	*Pieris rapae* Linnaeus
Green-veined White	*Pieris napi* Linnaeus
Bath White	*Pontia daplidice* Linnaeus
Orange Tip	*Anthocharis cardamines* Linnaeus

Family: LYCAENIDAE (The Blues, Coppers and Hairstreaks)

Sub-family: THECLINAE

Green Hairstreak	*Callophrys rubi* Linnaeus
Brown Hairstreak	*Thecla betulae* Linnaeus
Purple Hairstreak	*Quercusia quercus* Linnaeus
White-letter Hairstreak	*Strymonidia w-album* Knoch
Black Hairstreak	*Strymonidia pruni* Linnaeus

Sub-family: LYCAENINAE

Small Copper	*Lycaena phlaeas* Linnaeus
Large Copper	*Lycaena dispar* Haworth
Long-tailed Blue	*Lampides boeticus* Linnaeus
Small Blue	*Cupido minimus* Fuessly
Short-tailed Blue	*Everes argiades* Pallas
Silver-studded Blue	*Plebejus argus* Linnaeus
Brown Argus	*Aricia agestis* Denis and Schiffermüller
Northern Brown Argus	*Aricia artaxerxes* Fabricius
Common Blue	*Polyommatus icarus* Rottemburg
Chalk Hill Blue	*Lysandra coridon* Poda
Adonis Blue	*Lysandra bellargus* Rottemburg
Mazarine Blue	*Cyaniris semiargus* Rottemburg
Large Blue	*Maculinea arion* Linnaeus
Holly Blue	*Celastrina argiolus* Linnaeus

Family: NEMEOBIIDAE

Duke of Burgundy Fritillary	*Hamearis lucina* Linnaeus

Family: NYMPHALIDAE (The Vanessids and Fritillaries)

White Admiral	*Ladoga camilla* Linnaeus
Purple Emperor	*Apatura iris* Linnaeus
Red Admiral	*Vanessa atalanta* Linnaeus
Painted Lady	*Cynthia cardui* Linnaeus
Small Tortoiseshell	*Aglais urticae* Linnaeus
Large Tortoiseshell	*Nymphalis polychloros* Linnaeus
Peacock	*Inachis io* Linnaeus
Camberwell Beauty	*Nymphalis antiopa* Linnaeus
Comma	*Polygonia c-album* Linnaeus
Small Pearl-bordered Fritillary	*Boloria selene* Denis and Schiffermüller
Pearl-bordered Fritillary	*Argynnis euphrosyne* Linnaeus
Queen of Spain Fritillary	*Argynnis lathonia* Linnaeus
High Brown Fritillary	*Argynnis adippe* Denis and Schiffermüller
Dark Green Fritillary	*Argynnis aglaja* Linnaeus
Silver-washed Fritillary	*Argynnis paphia* Linnaeus

Marsh Fritillary	*Euphydryas aurinia* Rottemburg
Glanville Fritillary	*Melitaea cinxia* Linnaeus
Heath Fritillary	*Mellicta athalia* Rottemburg

Family: SATYRIDAE (The Browns)

Speckled Wood	*Pararge aegeria* Linnaeus
Wall	*Pararge megera* Linnaeus
Mountain Ringlet	*Erebia epiphron* Knoch
Scotch Argus	*Erebia aethiops* Esper
Marbled White	*Melanargia galathea* Linnaeus
Grayling	*Hipparchia semele* Linnaeus
Gatekeeper or Hedge Brown	*Maniola tithonus* Linnaeus
Meadow Brown	*Maniola jurtina* Linnaeus
Small Heath	*Coenonympha pamphilus* Linnaeus
Large Heath	*Coenonympha tullia* Müller
Ringlet	*Aphantopus hyperantus* Linnaeus

Family: DANAIDAE

Monarch or Milkweed	*Danaus plexippus* Linnaeus

10. *Societies to Join*

British Butterfly Conservation Society
Tudor House
Quorn
Leicestershire LE12 8AD

Amateur Entomologists' Society
Enrolment Secretary
3 Woodbourne
Farnham
Surrey GU9 9EF

British Entomological & Natural History Society
c/o The Alpine Club
74 South Audley Street
London WLY 5FF

Royal Entomological Society of London
41 Queens Gate
London SW7 5HU

County Naturalists' Trusts – details of your local Trusts are available from:

The Society for the Promotion of Nature Conservation
The Green
Nettleham
Lincoln LN2 2NR

BIBLIOGRAPHY

In writing this book, I consulted the following books and papers, some of which are not mentioned in the text.

ALBIN, ELEAZAR. *A Natural History of English Insects*. Published and printed by the author at his own expense, through subscription, and sold through William and John Innys, London, 1720.

BEAUFOY, S. *Butterfly Lives*. Collins, London, 1947.

BRISCOE, EDMUND. *Butterflies* (8th edition). Publisher unlisted, 1957.

BROWER, L. P. and BROWER, J. V. Z. Parallelism, convergence, divergence, and the new concept of advergence in the evolution of mimicry. *Transactions of the Connecticut Academy of Arts and Sciences*, vol. 44, pp. 57–67, 1972.

BROWER, L. P., BROWER, J. V. Z. and COLLINS, C. T. Experimental studies of mimicry, part 7. Relative palatability and Müllerian mimicry among neo-tropical butterflies of the sub-family Heliconiinones. *Zoologica*, New York, vol. 48, pp. 65–84, 1954.

BROWN, CAPTAIN THOMAS. *Brown's Butterflies, etc.* Vol. 1, 1832. One of 3 volumes called *The Book of Butterflies, Sphinxes and Moths*. Whittaker, Treacher & Co, Edinburgh, 1832–4.

BURTON, JOHN. A bumper year for butterflies. *Country Life*, pp. 1240–42, 25 October 1973.

CHALMERS-HUNT, J. M. The 1976 invasion of the Camberwell Beauty. *Entomologists' Record*, vol. 89, pp. 89–105; 248–9, 1977.

Chambers Twentieth-century Dictionary. Edited by A. M. Macdonald. W. and R. Chambers, London, 1972. Updated 1975.

COLEMAN, W. S. *British Butterflies with Coloured Illustrations*. Routledge, Warne and Routledge, New York, 1863.

CORNEILLE, THOMAS. *Dictionnaires des Arts et des Sciences*. 2 vols. Paris, 1694.

COX, MOLLY. *The Discoverers*. Television Project No. 3346/1603, 1975.

DARWIN, CHARLES ROBERT. *Voyage of Beagle 1832–36*. Also issued separately as *Journal and Researches into Geology and Natural History of Various Countries visited by H.M.S. Beagle*. Many editions, John Murray, Ward Lock, etc. Also issued as part of 3 vols. edited by P. P. King and others, called *Narrative of the Surveying Voyages of H.M.S. Adventure and Beagle*. Vol. 3. Journal and remarks by Charles Darwin.

DEMPSTER, J. P., with KING, M. L., and LAKHANI, K. H. The status of the Swallowtail butterfly in Britain. *Ecological Entomology*, vol. 1, pp. 71–84, 1976.

DUFFEY, ERIC. Ecological studies in the Large Copper butterfly *Lycaena dispar* Haw *batavus* Obth at Wood-walton Fen National Nature Reserve, Huntingdonshire. *Journal of Applied Ecology*, vol. 5, pp. 69–96, April 1968.

DUNCAN, JAMES. Memoir of Maria Sibilla Merian. In 'British Moths, Sphinxes, etc' edited by William Jardine. *The Naturalist Library*, vol. 30, 1835.

DUNCAN, JAMES. *British Butterflies.* W. H. Lizars, 1852.

Encyclopedia Britannica. 1970.

FELTWELL, J. S. E. The metabolism of carotenoids in *Pieris brassicae* L. (the Large White butterfly) in relation to its food plant *Brassica oleracea* var. *capita* L. (the cabbage). PhD thesis, Royal Holloway College, London, 1973.

FELTWELL, J. S. E. and VALADON, L. R. G. Carotenoids of *Pieris brassicae* L. and of its food plant. *Journal of Insect Physiology*, vol. 13, pp. 2203–15, 1972.

FORD, E. B. *Butterflies.* Collins, London, 1945.

FROHAWK, F. W. *Natural History of British Butterflies.* Hutchinson. Vol. 1 1913, vol. 2 1924.

FUNK and WAGNALL. *Standard Dictionary of Folklore, Mythology and Legend*, vol. 1. Mayflower (paperback), London, 1951.

GOODDEN, ROBERT, *Butterflies.* Hamlyn, 1971.

GOODDEN, ROBERT. *The Wonderful World of Butterflies and Moths.* Hamlyn, 1977.

GOODDEN, ROBERT and GOODDEN, ROSEMARY. Saving the Large Blue. *Country Life*, pp. 14–15, 4 July 1974.

GRIGSON, GEOFFREY. *The Shell Country Book.* Phoenix House Ltd, London, 1962.

HARRIS, MOSES. *The Aurelian.* Printed for the author, London, 1776.

HEAL, HENRY GEORGE. A summary of the work at Drum Manor. *The International Journal of Environmental Studies*, vol. 4, pp. 223–9, 1973.

HEATH, JOHN. *The Moths and Butterflies of Great Britain and Ireland.* Vol. 1. Curwen Press, London, 1976.

HEATH, JOHN. A century of change in the Lepidoptera. Systematics Association Special Volume no. 6. *The Changing Flora and Fauna of Great Britain*, edited by D. L. Hawksworth, pp. 275–92. Academic Press, London and New York, 1974.

HEATH, JOHN with PERRING, FRANKLYN. Biological recording in Europe. *Endeavour*, vol. 34, no. 123, September 1975.

HIGGINS, L. G. and RILEY, N. D. *A Field Guide to the Butterflies of Britain and Europe.* Collins, 1970.

HILL, J. *The Book of Nature, or The History of Insects.* C. G. Seyffert, London, 1758.

HOWARTH, T. G. *South's British Butterflies.* Frederick Warne, London, 1973.

HULME, F. EDWARD. *Butterflies and Moths of the Countryside.* Hutchinson, 1903.

HUXLEY, JULIAN. The Introduction to *The Beauty of Butterflies*, text by Adolf Portmann. B. T. Batsford, London, 1945.

JERMYN, LAETITIA (later known as Laetitia Jermyn Ford). *The Butterfly Collector's Vade Mecum.* J. Raw, Ipswich, 1827.

JOHNSON, C. G. *Migration and Dispersal of Insects by Flight.* Methuen, 1969.

KIRBY, W. F. *The Butterflies and Moths of Europe.* Cassell and Co. London, 1903.

KIRBY, W. F. and SPENCE, W. *An Introduction to Entomology or Elements of the Natural History of Insects.* 4 vols. Longman, Hurst, Rees, etc, London, 1815–26.

LANE, CHARLES. A note on the behaviour of the Meadow Brown (*Maniola jurtina* L.) (Lep. Satyridae) in Austria. *Entomologist's Monthly Magazine*, p. 220, 18 April 1962.

LANE, CHARLES. Insect migration on the north coast of France. *Entomologist's Monthly Magazine*, vol. 91, pp. 301–306, 3 January 1956.

LARSEN, TORBEN B. Three and a half millenia of *Danaus chrysippus* L. (Lepidoptera Danaidae) in Upper Egypt. *Linnéana Belgica*, vol. 7, pp. 55–8, 1 November 1977. (In French).

LEWIN, W. *The Papilios of Great Britain.* J. Johnson, 1795.

LIDDELL and SCOTT. *The Greek-English Lexicon.* J. H. and J. Parker, Oxford, 1843.

LINNAEUS, C. *Systema Naturae.* Edition decima. Holmiae. 1758.

MEASURES, DAVID. *Bright Wings of Summer.* Cassell, 1976.

MERIAN, MARIA. *The New Flower Book (Neues Blumenbuch allen Kunstverständigen Liebhabern zu Lust).* Nürnberg, 1680.

MERIAN, MARIA. *The Wonderful Formation of Caterpillars and Their Strange Diet of Flowers* (*Der Raupen Wunderbare Verwandelung und Sonderbare Blumen–Nährung*). Nürnberg, 1679–83.

MERRETT, CHRISTOPHER. *Pinax rerum Naturalium Britannicarum continens Vegetabilia, Animalia et Fossilia, in hac Insul reperta Inchoatus*. London, 1666.

MOFFETT, T. *Insectorum, sive Minimorum Animalium Theatrum etc.* Edited by T. de Mayerne. T. Cotes, London, 1634.

MORRIS, FRANCIS ORPEN. *A History of British Butterflies.* 1st edition. George Bell and Sons, London, 1853.

NEWMAN, EDWARD. *A Natural History of All the British Butterflies.* W. Tweedie, Edinburgh, 1860.

NEWMAN, EDWARD. *An Illustrated Natural History of British Butterflies.* W. Tweedie, Edinburgh, 1870.

NEWMAN, L. HUGH. *Living with Butterflies.* Billing and Sons, London, 1967. (First published 1953 as *Butterfly Farmer.*)

NEWMAN, L. HUGH and SAVONIUS, MOIRA. *Create a Butterfly Garden.* John Baker, 1967.

Oxford English Dictionary. Edited by Sir J. A. H. Murray. Oxford University Press, 1971.

PETIVER, J. *Papilionum Britanniae Icones, Nomina etc.* Included as part 6 in vol. 2. *Opera Historia Naturalem Spectantia.* John Millan, London, 1767.

POLLARD, E. with ELIAS, D. O., SKELTON, M. J. and THOMAS, J. A. A method of assessing the abundance of butterflies in Monks Wood Nature Reserve in 1973. *Entomologist's Gazette,* vol. 26, pp. 79–106, 1975.

POLLARD, E., HOOPER, M. D. and MOORE, N. W. *Hedges.* New Naturalist 58, Collins, 1974.

PYLE, ROBERT. The scientific management of butterfly and moth populations; a new thrust of wildlife conservation. *Discovery,* vol. 11, no. 2, pp. 69–77, 1976.

PYLE, ROBERT. The eco-graphic basis for Lepidoptera conservation. *Dissertation Abstracts International,* vol. 37, no. 7, p. 3254, 1977.

RAY, JOHN. *Historia Insectorum.* A. and J. Churchill, London, 1790.

RILEY, N. D. *Department of the British Museum (Natural History). A brief historical sketch, 1904–64.* Proceedings of the 12th International Congress of Entomology, 1964.

RILEY, N. D. *A Code for Insect Collecting.* The Joint Committee for the Conservation of British Insects. Undated.

ROTHSCHILD, MIRIAM. Mimicry: the deceptive way of life. *Natural History,* vol. 76, pp. 44–51, February 1967.

ROTHSCHILD, MIRIAM. Assessment of eggs laid by *Pieris brassicae* (Lepidoptera Pieridae). *Nature,* vol. 266, no. 5600, pp. 352–5, 24 March 1977.

ROTHSCHILD, MIRIAM, REICHSTEIN, T., VON EUW, J. and PARSONS, J. A. Heart poisons in the Monarch butterfly. *Science,* vol. 161, pp. 861–6, 30 August 1968.

ROTHSCHILD, MIRIAM and FORD, BOB. Heart poisons and the Monarch. *Natural History,* vol. 79, pp. 36–8, April 1970.

SALANSKY, FRANK. Cardiac glycosides in *Esclepias* species. *Journal of the Lepidopterists' Society,* vol. 26, p. 219, June 1972.

SANDARS, EDMUND. *A Butterfly Book for the Pocket.* Oxford University Press, 1939.

SHAW, GEORGE and NODDER, FREDERICK P. *Naturalist's Miscellany* vol. 5. Frederick P. Nodder, 1793–4.

SOUTH, R. *British Butterflies.* Frederick Warne, London, 1906.

STAINTON, HENRY TIBBATS. *British Butterflies and Moths.* Lovell Reeve, London, 1867.

STEELE, R. C. and WELCH, R. C. (editors). *Monks Wood. A Nature Reserve Record.* The Nature Conservancy, 1973.

STEPHENS, J. F. *Illustrations of British Entomology.* Baldwin and Craddock, 1828–35.

STOKOE, W. J. *The Observer's Book of Butterflies.* Frederick Warne, London, 1969.

STOKOE, W. J. and STOVIN, G. H. T. *The Caterpillars of British Butterflies* (based on *British Butterflies* by R. South). Frederick Warne, London, 1944.

SWAIN, H. D. *British Butterfly Identification Chart.* Frederick Warne, London, 1970.

SWAMMERDAM, J. J. *Historia Insectorum Generalis.* Utrecht, 1669.

THOMAS, J. A. The Hairstreaks of Monks Wood. In *Monks Wood. A Nature Reserve Record.* The Nature Conservancy, 1973.

TOPSEL, EDWARD and MUFFET, T. *The History of Animals, Serpents, etc.* (Sub-titled 'The History of Four-footed Beasts, Serpents and Insects'.) Printed by E. Cotes and M. Sawbridge at the Bible on Ludgate Hill, T. Williams at the Bible in Little Britain, and T. Johnson at the Key in Paul's Churchyard, 1658.

URQUHART, F. A. *The Monarch Butterfly.* University of Toronto Press, 1960.

URQUHART, F. A. A discussion of the use of the word 'migration' as it relates to a proposed classification for animal movements. Contributions of the Royal Ontario Museum Division of Zoology and Paleontology, Toronto, no. 50, 22 May 1958.

URQUHART, F. A. Found at last. The Monarch's winter home. *National Geographic Magazine,* vol. 150, no. 2, pp. 161–73. National Geographic Society, August 1976.

URQUHART, F. A. and URQUHART, N. R. Migration of butterflies along the Gulf Coast of northern Florida. *Journal of the Lepidopterists' Society,* vol. 18, no. 1, pp. 59–61, April 1976.

URQUHART, F. A., URQUHART, N. R. and MUNGER, F. A study of a continuously breeding population of *Danaus plexippus* (in southern California, compared to a migratory population, and its significance in the study of insect movement). *Journal of Research on Lepidoptera,* 1968.

WALEY, ARTHUR. *Three Ways of Thought of Ancient China* (translated from the Chinese). Allen and Unwin, 1939.

WERNER, ALFRED. *Butterflies and Moths.* André Deutsch, London, 1956.

WESTWOOD, J. O. (James Obadiah). *Arcana Entomologica or Illustrations of New, Rare and Interesting Insects.* William Smith, London, 1841–5.

WHITE, GILBERT. *The Natural History of Selborne.* (First published as *The Natural History and Antiquities of Selborne in the County of Southampton, with Engravings and an Appendix.*) B. White and Son at Horace's Head, Fleet Street, 1789.

WILKES, BENJAMIN. *One Hundred and Twenty Copperplates of English Moths and Butterflies.* B. White, 1773.

WILLIAMS, C. B. *Migration of Butterflies.* Oliver and Boyd, 1930.

WILLIAMS, C. B. *Insect Migration.* Collins, 1958.

INDEX

INDEX OF BUTTERFLIES

The first page reference is to the main details given of each butterfly.   **Bold** figures indicate illustrations.

INDEX OF PLACES AND PEOPLE

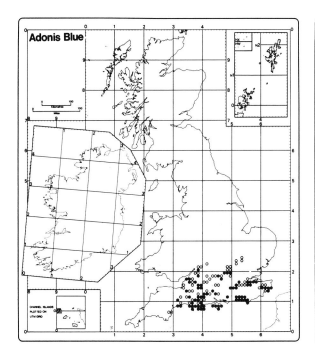

Adonis Blue

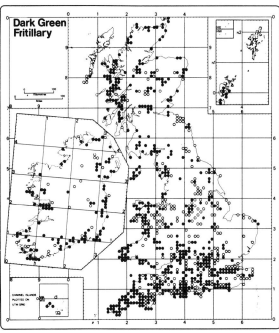

Dark Green Fritillary

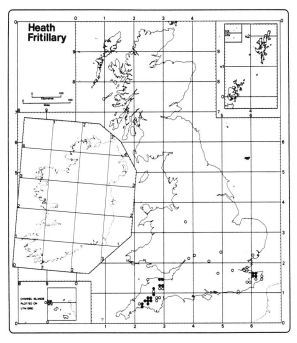

Heath Fritillary

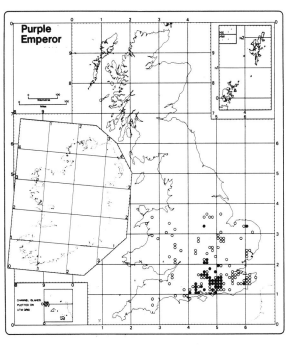

Purple Emperor

SELECTED DISTRIBUTION MAPS

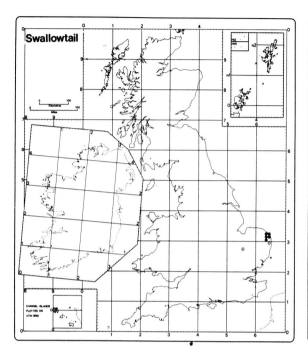

Swallowtail

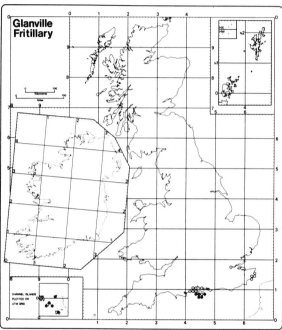

Glanville Fritillary

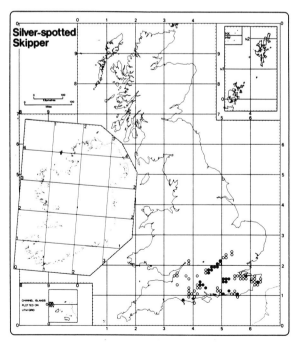

Silver-spotted Skipper

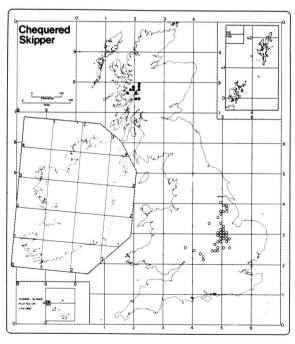

Chequered Skipper

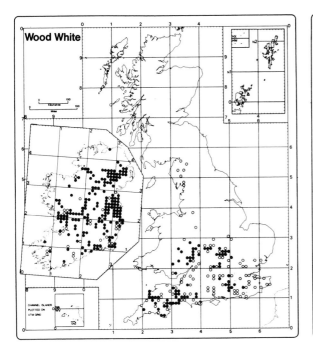

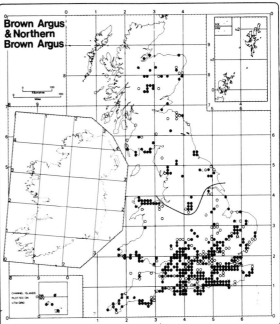